Guide to Professional Accounting Standards

Guide to Professional Accounting Standards

E. *James Meddaugh, Ph.D., C.P.A.*
Rochester Institute of Technology

PRENTICE-HALL, INC., ENGLEWOOD CLIFFS, N.J. 07632

Library of Congress Cataloging in Publication Data

MEDDAUGH, E. JAMES.
  Guide to professional accounting standards.

  1. Accounting—Standards—United States.
I. Title.
HF5657.M4   657'.0218   82-5306
ISBN 0-13-370700-8   AACR2

Editorial/production supervision and interior design by Pam Price
Cover design by Ray Lundgren
Manufacturing buyer: Ray Keating

Printed in the United States of America
10 9 8 7 6 5 4 3 2 1

ISBN 0-13-370700-8

Prentice-Hall International, Inc., London
Prentice-Hall of Australia Pty. Limited, Sydney
Prentice-Hall Canada Inc., Toronto
Prentice-Hall of India Private Limited, New Delhi
Prentice-Hall of Japan, Inc., Tokyo
Prentice-Hall of Southeast Asia Pte. Ltd., Singapore
Whitehall Books Limited, Wellington, New Zealand

Contents

GENERAL STANDARDS

Contents

Contents

GUIDE SECTION LOCATOR
Accounting Research Bulletins

APB Opinions

*Superseded by subsequent pronouncement

Contents

FASB Statements

*Superseded by subsequent pronouncement

FASB Interpretations

*Superseded by subsequent pronouncement

Preface

This *Guide to Professional Accounting Standards* is a working guide to all official pronouncements of the Committee on Accounting Procedure, the Accounting Principles Board, and the Financial Accounting Standards Board that were in effect on July 1, 1982. The Guide is a synopsis of the official accounting pronouncements which are published in complete form by the Financial Accounting Standards Board in two volumes entitled *Accounting Standards—Original Pronouncements* and *Accounting Standards—Current Text*. The Guide does not deal with all of the arguments, rationale, and appendices that are included in *Accounting Standards* but instead presents the essence of the official literature in a concise form. Use of the Guide thus presumes knowledge of the standards or at least familiarity with the fact that a pronouncement has been issued for a particular topic.

Accounting pronouncements are issued so frequently that it has become almost impossible to remember the current status for the many topics covered by the official accounting literature. The Guide is designed to be a ready reference source that can be carried easily to the classroom or in the field. Organization of the Guide follows that of *Accounting Standards—Current Text* for two reasons. First, practicing accountants increasingly are using current text versions of the pronouncements for reference because original pronouncements have been altered by subsequent pronouncements. The organization of the Guide thus facilitates easy reference to the more complete text of *Accounting Standards*. In the second place, students will become accustomed to the referencing scheme of *Accounting Standards* by using the Guide.

The format of each section of the Guide includes a sketch of the official literature including the following information:

1. FASB *Accounting Standards—Current Text* section number

2. References to the original pronouncements included:
   a. Accounting Research Bulletins
   b. APB Opinions
   c. FASB Statements of Financial Accounting Standards
   d. FASB Interpretations
   e. FASB Technical Bulletins
3. Brief profile of the pronouncements
4. Brief description of disclosure requirements

For most sections of the Guide the lead sketch is followed by a detailed synopsis of all requirements called for by the pronouncements. Certain small pronouncements are covered in the profile.

A special feature of the Guide is a cross-reference system which permits easy location of Guide sections when only the number of an original pronouncement is known by the user. For example, if one wanted to find APB Opinion 16, the Locator of APB Opinions indicates that this is covered in Section B50. The Locators for Accounting Research Bulletins, APB Opinions, FASB Statements, and FASB Interpretations are found following the Contents.

Acknowledgments

I would like to thank those people who provided help, encouragement, and constructive criticism during the time the Guide was being written:

Thanks to Ron Ledwith of Prentice-Hall, who helped me bring into focus the concept upon which the approach taken in the Guide was based.

Thanks to the following academic accountants who reviewed the complete manuscript and offered detailed suggestions on various sections of the text:

Prof. Michael A. Diamond, California State University—Los Angeles
Prof. Richard J. Murdock, Ohio State University
Prof. Alfred R. Roberts, Georgia State University

Thanks to my colleagues from public accounting in Rochester, New York who were willing to spend the time to reveiw Guide sections that I requested of them:

Virginia G. Hohman, Deloitte, Haskins & Sells
David M. Lang, Jr., Price Waterhouse & Co.
Edward L. Short, Coopers & Lybrand
James T. Sorensen, Peat, Marwick, Mitchell & Co.
Robert J. Wood, Metzger, Wood & Sokolski

A special note of thanks goes to Robert C. Wilkins, Project Manager at the Financial Accounting Standards Board, for his help in the rearrangement of this manuscript into the new topical outline adopted by the FASB when the Board decided to publish a new current text to replace the AICPA's *Professional Standards: Accounting— Current Text*.

Finally, my heartfelt appreciation goes to my wife, Dotty, and my daughters, Karen and Nancy, for putting up with me and my almost incessant chatter about "my book."

Sources for this topic in FASB *Accounting Standards: Current Text*:

APB Opinions 8, 20

FASB Statements 32, 56

FASB Interpretations 1, 20

PROFILE:

APB Opinion 20:

- Change in accounting principle: cumulative effect.
- Change in accounting estimate: prospective.
- Change in entity: restate prior financial statements.
- Correction of an error: prior period adjustment.

FASB Statements 32 and 56

- The FASB has indicated by Statement 32 that, until specific FASB Statements are issued to the contrary, special industry accounting and reporting presented in certain AICPA publications are preferable for purposes of applying APB Opinion 20. The list on the following pages, Appendix A from FASB 32, is a complete list of the AICPA publications containing preferable specialized industry accounting and reporting principles.
- The FASB added three AICPA documents to the list with FASB 56.

DISCLOSURE:

- Each of the changes requires different disclosure; see the text following.

APB Opinion 20

This opinion deals with three types of accounting changes and the reporting requirements for the correction of an error.

Change in Accounting Principle

Once adopted, accounting principles used by an entity for similar transactions should not be changed unless the change can be justified on grounds that the new principle is preferable (i.e., more clearly reflects income). Creation of a new accounting principle, indication of a preference for an accounting principle, or rejection of a specific principle by the FASB is justification for a change, whereas all other changes must be justified by the entity proposing the change.

Reporting a change in accounting principle: With three specific exceptions, changes in accounting principle should be accomplished in the financial statements for the year of the change. This means that:

1. Prior period statements remain as originally issued except for the addition of pro forma restatement of income before extraordinary items and net income figures.
2. The cumulative effect of changing to the new principle as of the beginning of the year of the change is included on the income statement (net of tax) after extraordinary items.
3. Operating income is determined using the new principle.

It is important to note that adoption of a different amortization method for all new acquisitions of long-lived assets in a particular category is not deemed to be a change in principle requiring cumulative effect adjustment as long as a change is not made for existing assets.

Exceptions to the general rule for reporting a change in accounting principle are:

1. A change from LIFO for inventory valuation to another method
2. A change from completed contract to percentage of completion for long-term construction contracts (and vice versa)
3. A change to or from the full-cost method of accounting in the extractive industries

In these specific circumstances financial statements of all prior years presented should be restated using the new principle. The cumulative effect on prior years of retroactively applying the new principle is reported as an adjustment to the beginning balance of retained earnings for each period presented.

Disclosure following a change in accounting principle shall include the nature of the change, the justification for the change, and the effect on income and earnings per share in the period of the change.

Change in Accounting Estimate

A change in accounting estimate should be reported prospectively, that is, for the period of the change and any subsequent periods affected. A change in estimate made simultaneously with a change in accounting principle should be reported as a change in estimate. In the case where the joint change involves a change in depreciation, depletion, or amortization methods, the effects of the two changes should be separated with the change in method treated as a change in principle and the change in estimate treated prospectively.

Disclosure is necessary for changes in estimates that affect several future periods. The effect on income before extraordinary items, net income, and related per share amounts is required for such changes.

Change in Entity

Reporting a change in entity requires restatement of financial statements for all periods presented to present comparable information for the entity as it exists at the most recent date.

Disclosure should include a description of the change and the reason for the change as well as the effect on income before extraordinary items, net income, and the related per share amounts for all periods presented.

Correction of an Error

Correction of an error should be reported as a prior period adjustment (adjustment to beginning retained earnings; see Sec. A35).

Disclosure should include the nature of the error previously made and the effect of correcting it on the income before extraordinary items, net income, and related per share amounts.

Interpretation 1

Changes in the composition of elements of cost included in inventory is an accounting change and thus subject to the rules cited above.

Interpretation 20

An entity making a change to conform with an AICPA Statement of Position shall report the change as specified in that Statement. If the Statement does not specify how to report the change, APB Opinion 20 should be followed.

FASB Statement 32

The following AICPA publications contain specialized industry accounting and reporting principles considered to be preferable for purposes of applying APB Opinion 20.

Statements of Position*

SOP 74-6	Recognition of Profit on Sales of Receivables with Recourse
SOP 74-8	Financial Accounting and Reporting by Colleges and Universities
SOP 74-11	Financial Accounting and Reporting by Face-Amount Certificate Companies
SOP 74-12	Accounting Practices in the Mortgage Banking Industry
SOP 75-2	Accounting Practices of Real Estate Investment Trusts
SOP 75-5	Accounting Practices in the Broadcasting Industry
SOP 75-6	Questions Concerning Profit Recognition on Sales of Real Estate
SOP 76-2	Accounting for Origination Costs and Loan and Commitment Fees in the Mortgage Banking Industry
SOP 76-3	Accounting Practices for Certain Employee Stock Ownership Plans
SOP 77-1	Financial Accounting and Reporting by Investment Companies

*The following lists are from the *Statement of Financial Accounting Standards No. 32*, Financial Accounting Standards Board, 1979, pp. 7-9. Copyright by the Financial Accounting Standards Board, High Ridge Park, Stamford, Connecticut 06905 U.S.A. Reprinted with permission. Copies of the complete document are available from the FASB.

SOP 78-1	Accounting by Hospitals for Certain Marketable Equity Securities
SOP 78-2	Accounting Practices of Real Estate Investment Trusts
SOP 78-3	Accounting for Costs to Sell and Rent, and Initial Rental Operations of, Real Estate Projects
SOP 78-4	Application of the Deposit, Installment, and Cost Recovery Methods in Accounting for Sales of Real Estate
SOP 78-5	Accounting for Advance Refundings of Tax-Exempt Debt
SOP 78-7	Financial Accounting and Reporting by Hospitals Operated by a Governmental Unit
SOP 78-9	Accounting for Investments in Real Estate Ventures
SOP 78-10	Accounting Principles and Reporting Practices for Certain Nonprofit Organizations
SOP 79-1	Accounting for Municipal Bond Funds
SOP 81-1	Accounting for Performance of Construction-Type and Certain Production-Type Contracts
SOP 81-2	Reporting Practices Concerning Hospital-Related Organizations

Industry Accounting Guides

Accounting for Profit Recognition on Sales of Real Estate, 1973 (see also SOPs 75-6 and 78-4)

Accounting for Retail Land Sales, 1973

Industry Audit Guides

Audits of Banks, Including Supplement, 1969

Audits of Brokers and Dealers in Securities, 1973

Audits of Colleges and Universities, 1973 (see also SOP 74-8)

Audits of Employee Health and Welfare Benefit Funds, 1972

Audits of Finance Companies, 1973

Audits of Government Contractors, 1975

Audits of Investment Companies, 1973 (see also SOPs 74-11, 77-1, and 79-1)

Audits of Personal Financial Statements, 1968

Audits of Voluntary Health and Welfare Organizations, 1974

Hospital Audit Guide, 1972 (see also SOPs 78-1 and 78-7)

Audit and Accounting Guides

Construction Contractors

Savings and Loan Associations

Sources for this topic in FASB *Accounting Standards: Current Text*:
  APB Opinion 22

PROFILE:
  • When financial statements are issued (singly or complete
    set), a description of the issuer's important account-
    ing policies is required. This requirement applies to
    both profit-oriented and not-for-profit entities. Dis-
    closures are not required for interim reports if poli-
    cies have not changed since the last annual report.

DISCLOSURE:
  • Disclosure should include identification, description, and
    methods of application of accounting principles that
    materially affect the financial statements. Specific
    disclosures are required for:
    1. Reasons for selection from alternative principles
    2. Principles peculiar to the industry
    3. Unusual applications of principles
  • A partial list of disclosures normally required concern:
    1. Basis of consolidation
    2. Depreciation methods
    3. Amortization of intangibles
    4. Inventory pricing
    5. Recognition of revenue on construction contracts
    6. Recognition of revenue from franchises and leases

Sources for this topic in FASB *Accounting Standards: Current Text*:
  ARB 43, Chap. 1A

PROFILE:

- Capital surplus must not absorb charges which are properly chargeable against income. This rule is not to be construed as a prohibition of quasi-reorganizations.

Sources for this topic in FASB *Accounting Standards: Current Text*:

APB Opinions 9, 20

FASB Statement 16

PROFILE:

- Prior period adjustments should be reported as adjustments to beginning retained earnings.
- Prior period adjustments include only corrections of errors and adjustments for certain operating loss carryforwards.

DISCLOSURE:

- Disclosure depends on how many periods are presented and the period to which the adjustment applies; see the text for details.

APB Opinion 9

Prior period adjustments should be reported as adjustments to the beginning balance of retained earnings, such as:

Retained earnings, Jan. 1, 1980, as reported	$XX,XXX
Less prior period adjustment (Note X)	XXX
Revised retained earnings, Jan. 1, 1980	$XX,XXX

When comparative statements are issued, the effects of the prior period adjustment should be distributed retroactively throughout all statements presented and, if necessary, any remaining amounts that relate to periods earlier than the earliest year presented should be made as adjustments to the earliest beginning retained earnings figure as displayed above.

Disclosure: In the year in which a prior period adjustment is recorded, the financial statements shall disclose the effects, both gross and net of tax, that the item has on net income of prior years. When only one year is presented, the effects on beginning retained earnings as well as the effects on net income of the prior year should be disclosed.

FASB Statement 16

All items of profit and loss should be included in income except for prior period adjustments. Prior period adjustments have been redefined to include only:

1. Corrections of errors made in the financial statements of prior years
2. Realization of operating loss carryforwards that existed (but were not accounted for) prior to the acquisition of purchased subsidiaries

Sources for this topic in FASB *Accounting Standards: Current Text*:

ARB 43, Chap. 3A
APB Opinion 6
FASB Statement 6
FASB Interpretation 8
FASB Technical Bulletin 79-3

PROFILE:

- Current assets and liabilities, which are determinants of working capital, should be classified with reference to the operating cycle or a year, whichever is longer. Assets that will be sold or consumed during the normal operating cycle should be classified as current. Liabilities that will be paid during the operating cycle should be classified as current.

- Short-term obligations expected to be refinanced may be excluded from current liabilities *only if* both intent and ability to refinance exist.

DISCLOSURE:

- Notes to the financial statements should present details of the agreement to refinance.

FASB Statement 6

Short-term obligations expected to be refinanced on a long-term basis may be excluded from current liabilities if both the intent and the ability to refinance exist at the balance sheet date.

The ability to refinance is determined by either:

1. Actual refinancing after the balance sheet date, or
2. Entering into an agreement to refinance after the balance sheet date. The agreement should extend beyond one year, not be violated at (or subsequent to) the balance sheet date, and the prospective lender must have the ability to consummate the agreement.

Exclusion from current liabilities should not exceed the received or expected proceeds from refinancing.

Notes to the financial statements should include a description of the financing agreement and the terms of the new obligation or equity securities involved.

Interpretation 8

Short-term obligations should not be excluded from current liabilities when paid subsequent to the balance sheet date and a long-term obligation is issued subsequently to restore current assets used to retire the short-term obligation.

Sources for this topic in FASB *Accounting Standards: Current Text*:

    ARB 43, Chap. 1A

    ARB 51

    APB Opinion 16

    FASB Statements 10, 38

    FASB Interpretations 4, 9, 25

    FASB Technical Bulletin 81–2

PROFILE:

APB Opinion 16:

- Purchase and pooling methods are both acceptable, but the facts in each case will indicate which is required.
- Pooling requires continued accountability for acquired firm.
- Purchase requires a new accountability based on fair values.

FASB Statement 10:

- APB Opinion 16 contained a provision that companies could still qualify for pooling-of-interest accounting for a business combination if they had more than a 10% intercorporate investment when the Opinion became effective and if they completed a business combination with the investee before the five-year period ending October 31, 1975, expired.
- This FASB Statement removed the five-year limitation, thus extending the "grandfather" period indefinitely.

FASB Statement 38:

- Preacquisition contingencies (contingent assets, contingent liabilities, and contingent impairment of assets) shall be included in the allocation of the purchase price of acquirees:

  1. At fair value if determinable in the "allocation period," or

  2. At a reasonable estimate if it is probable by the end of the "allocation period" that the contingency is real

- Adjustments required beyond the allocation period shall be taken to income of the adjustment period.
- The "allocation period" is a period of time subsequent to the business combination, not exceeding one year, during which information is collected for identifying and quantifying the assets and liabilities of the acquired entity.

DISCLOSURE:

- Detailed information about each business combination must be disclosed in the year a combination takes place. Other supplemental pro forma disclosures may also be required; see the text following.

APB Opinion 16

This opinion specifies conditions when business combinations should be accounted for using the purchase method and the pooling-of-interests method. Both of these methods are acceptable, but they are not alternatives for the same transaction. If the specified conditions for a pooling are met, the combination must be accounted for using the pooling method; otherwise, purchase accounting is required.

The conditions that must be met for a pooling fall into three categories:

1. Characteristics of the constituent companies
2. Methods used to effect the combination
3. Existence of plans to circumvent the other requirements

Each of the twelve specific conditions must be met for a combination to be properly be classified as a pooling.

Characteristics of the Constituent Companies

1. The companies must be autonomous and must not have been a subsidiary or division of another firm for at least two years before the combination.
2. The companies must be independent of each other but incorporate investments of up to 10% of the common stock of the other party is acceptable.

Methods Used to Effect the Combination

3. The combination is accomplished in one transaction or results from a plan within one year from the time it is initiated.

4. One party issues common stock in exchange for at least 90% of the outstanding common stock of the other party.

5. None of the constituent companies changes the equity interest of its common stock in anticipation of the combination within two years before the combination or between initiation and completion of the plan for combination.

6. Treasury shares are acquired only for purposes unrelated to the business combination, such as stock option and compensation plans.

7. The relative interests of individual stockholders remain the same as they were before the exchange of stock.

8. Voting rights of common shares of the combined company are not restricted in any way.

9. The combination is completed at the final date of the plan and there are no contingencies related to issuance of securities to effect the combination.

Existence of Plans to Circumvent the Other Requirements

10. There is no agreement to retire or reacquire any shares issued to effect the combination.

11. There are no other financial arrangements to benefit former stockholders of a combining company.

12. There is no plan to dispose of a major portion of the assets of a combined company within two years after the combination other than normal business disposals or disposal of duplicate facilities.

Application of the Pooling Method

Accounting bases of the constituent companies continue in the combined company as if the companies had always been combined. In other words, there is no new basis of accountability in a pooling. The following items demonstrate the essence of a pooling on the accounts and financial statements.

1. Assets and liabilities are combined from the constituent companies at book value.

2. Capital and retained earnings accounts are also combined. If the total par value of shares issued by the combined company is greater than the par value of the shares of the combining companies, the difference should first be deducted from the combined paid in capital in excess of par and only if this is insufficient should amounts be deducted from retained earnings.

3. Untainted treasury shares used to effect the combination (i.e., acquired more than two years before the combination) should be accounted for as if retired and then newly issued.

4. Results of operations for the year of the combination should be reported as if the companies were combined at the beginning of the year except that intercompany transactions during the period of the year prior to the combination should be eliminated.

5. Balance sheets as of the beginning of the period of combination and all prior periods presented should be restated as if the companies were combined at those dates. These pro forma statements should clearly indicate that the data are from previously separate companies.

6. All costs of the business combination should be expensed in the year the combination took place. This includes finder's fees, costs of issuing securities, and costs of merging the operations.

7. Disposal of duplicate or excess facilities within two years of the combination requires reporting as an extraordinary item, net of tax.

Disclosure for a Pooling

For the period in which a pooling combination occurred, notes to the financial statements should include information concerning the following seven items.

1. The name and a brief description of the companies combined

2. A statement that the pooling method was used to account for the combination

3. Number and description of the shares issued to combine the companies

4. Information about operations for each company for the period of the year prior to the combination, including revenue, extraordinary items, net income, changes in stockholders' equity, and intercompany transactions

5. Information about adjustments made to change accounting methods for any constituent to bring accounting methods to the same basis

6. Information regarding the effect on retained earnings of changing the fiscal year for a combining company

7. Reconciliation of previously reported revenue and earnings with the combined amounts

Application of the Purchase Method

Cost of the acquired company is the cash or fair value of other assets distributed, the present value of debt issued, or in the case of stock issued, the fair value of the company acquired. If the stock issued to effect the combination is regularly traded, the quoted market value may be used to approximate the fair value of the acquired company after taking into account the market price for a reasonable period before and after the merger announcement.

Cost should also include the direct costs of the acquisition, such as finder's fees and legal fees. Costs of issuing securities, however, should be recorded as a reduction in the proceeds of issuing those securities.

Contingent consideration is usually additional cost when distributed unless the contingency was related only to security prices, in which case rearrangement of equity accounts is the proper treatment when additional shares are issued.

Recording of assets and liabilities should be at fair value as determined as of the date of the combination. Any excess of cost over total fair value should be recorded as goodwill. An excess of total fair value over cost indicates a bargain purchase and this excess should be distributed as a pro rata reduction of noncurrent assets exclusive of marketable securities. If noncurrent assets are brought to zero by this pro rata distribution, any remaining difference should be set up as a deferred credit and systematically amortized to income.

Disclosure for a Purchase

For the period in which a purchase combination occurred, notes to the financial statements should include information concerning the following six items.

1. Name and brief description of the acquired company
2. An indication that the purchase method of accounting is used
3. The period of operations of the acquired company which are included in the acquiring company's income statement
4. Cost of the acquired company and the number of, and amount assigned to, shares issued to effect the combination
5. Description of the method and period for amortization of goodwill
6. Description of contingencies and proposed accounting on their settlement

Supplemental pro forma information should also be presented for the current period (and prior period if comparative statements are issued), indicating results of operations as if the companies had been combined as of the beginning of the period(s).

Interpretation 4

When assets acquired in a purchase business combination are to be used for research and development, they must be accounted for in the same manner as they would be with any other acquisition method. The cost of such assets is their cost to the acquiring entity, not the cost to the acquired entity.

Interpretation 9

Deals with purchase accounting when used with acquisition of a savings and loan association. Conclusions were:

1. Net-spread method of assigning values to assets and liabilities ignores fair values and is thus unacceptable.
2. Reaffirms the position of APB Opinion 17 that straight-line amortization of goodwill is required unless the firm can demonstrate that another method is more appropriate.

Sources for this topic in FASB *Accounting Standards: Current Text*:
    ARB 43, Chap. 1A
    APB Opinions 9, 12, 14, 19

PROFILE:

- When complete financial statements are presented, disclosure of changes in each stockholders equity account and changes in the number of shares shall be made for at least the most recent fiscal year. Such changes are also required for any subsequent interim period presented.

- When stock is issued for property and some of the stock is immediately donated back to the issuing corporation, the cost of the property must not be recorded at the par value of the original number of shares issued. Further, if these donated shares are resold, the proceeds must not be included in surplus.

DISCLOSURE:

- Changes in equity accounts may be disclosed in a separate statement, in the body of the basic financial statements, or in the footnotes.

Sources for this topic in FASB *Accounting Standards: Current Text*:
APB Opinion 29

PROFILE

- Transfer of a nonmonetary asset in a nonreciprocal transfer should be recorded at the fair value of the asset surrendered with appropriate recognition of gain or loss.

Sources for this topic in FASB *Accounting Standards: Current Text*:
   APB Opinions 10, 15

PROFILE:

- When preferred stock has a liquidation value substantially
     in excess of par or stated value, this information
     must be disclosed on the balance sheet. In addition,
     the balance sheet or notes must include:
   1. Total or per share call price
   2. Total and per share cumulative dividends in arrears

Sources for this topic in FASB *Accounting Standards: Current Text*:
ARB 43, Chap. 7B; ARB 51

PROFILE:

- Stock dividends shall be recorded by capitalizing the fair value of shares issued.
- Stock splits shall not have retained earnings capitalized.
- Recipients of shares from stock splits or stock dividends must not record income but shall allocate the book value to all shares owned.

Receipt of shares by an investor from a stock dividend or stock split are not income. Rather, the cost of the investment is represented by a larger number of shares and the book value per share should be adjusted accordingly.

Acounting for stock dividends and stock splits by the issuing entity, regardless of the label given to the transaction by the entity, depends on the relative size of the increase in shares.

1. Shares issued are less than 20 to 25% of existing shares: the dividend shall be recorded by charging retained earnings for the fair value of the shares issued.

2. Shares issued are more than 25% of existing shares: no amount of retained earnings shall be capitalized.

Sources for this topic in FASB *Accounting Standards: Current Text*:

    ARB 43, Chaps. 1A, 1B
    APB Opinion 6

PROFILE:

- Profit or loss shall not be recorded on transactions in an entity's own shares.
- Retirement of shares generally affects paid-in capital and only rarely is retained earnings reduced.
- Dividends shall not be recorded (and income shall not be affected) for shares of its own stock that a corporation holds as treasury stock (even if that stock is carried as an asset).

DISCLOSURE:

- Restrictions on the payment of dividends must be disclosed.

Profit or loss shall not be recognized on the acquisition or disposal of treasury stock. When treasury stock is acquired it may be carried at cost as a deduction from stockholders' equity (retirement of the shares has not been decided) or the shares may be retired.

When treasury shares are retired, an excess of the par or stated value of the shares over the reacquisition price shall be reported as additional paid-in capital (never retained earnings). When the reacquisition price exceeds the par or stated value of the shares, the charges to retire the shares shall be distributed as follows:

1. Par or stated value should be eliminated.
2. All paid-in capital from previous treasury stock transactions for the same issue and a proportionate part of all other paid-in capital accounts for the same issue may be eliminated.
3. Any additional amounts must be charged to retained earnings.

An alternative to the second and third steps is to charge the total excess over par or stated value to retained earnings.

When payment of dividends is restricted by state law because of the treasury stock, this restriction must be disclosed.

Sources for this topic in FASB *Accounting Standards: Current Text*:

FASB Statements 33, 39, 40, 41, 46, 54

FASB Technical Bulletins 79-8, 81-4

PROFILE:

- Only largest companies are required to comply with FASB 33.

- Supplemental information regarding inventories and fixed assets (and related cost expiration) must be provided with the usual financial statements.

- Supplemental information must be measured in terms of *both* constant dollars and current costs.

- FASB Statements 39, 40, 41, 46 and 54 amend the requirements of FASB Statement 33 for certain specialized industries. See the text following.

DISCLOSURE:

- May be at a minimum level or may be complete financial statements. All disclosures are supplemental to historical cost financial statements.

FASB Statement 33

This statement is experimental and applies only to the largest companies. The requirements of the statement do not alter generally accepted accounting principles for primary financial statements. All requirements are supplementary to annual reports that contain the primary statements; the supplementary information is not required for interim statements (although presumably permissible), and the supplementary information is not required for segments (although explicitly encouraged).

Constant dollar and current cost information is required only for inventory and fixed assets and the related income statement effect of the changes in these assets. All other accounts may be left at historical cost.

Largest Firms

Companies meeting *either* of the following tests, based on figures from their primary financial statements, are required to comply with this statement:

1. The sum of inventories and gross property, plant, and equipment exceeds $125 million.
2. Total assets net of depreciation exceed $1 billion.

A one-year exemption, the year in which a business combination occurs, is granted when none of the constituents to a pooling of interests meets this test.

Summary of Required Disclosures

1. For the current year:
   a. Historical cost/constant dollar basis:
      (1) Information relative to income from continuing operations (exclusive of the purchasing power gain or loss)
      (2) Purchasing power gain or loss on net monetary items
   b. Current cost basis:
      (1) Information relative to income from continuing operations (exclusive of the change in item 3 below)
      (2) Current cost of inventory and plant, property, and equipment at year-end
      (3) Change in current cost over the year, adjusted for

inflation, of inventory and plant, property, and equipment

c. In notes to this current information:
   (1) Types (sources) of information used to determine current costs
   (2) Differences in depreciation methods, useful lives, or salvage values between supplemental disclosures and primary financial statements
   (3) Explanation of differences in tax expense between supplemental and primary financial information

2. For the five most recent years:
   a. Net sales and other operating revenues
   b. Historical cost/constant dollar information:
      (1) Income from continuing operations
      (2) Income per common share from continuing operations
      (3) Net assets at fiscal year-end
   c. Current cost information:
      (1) Income from continuing operations
      (2) Income per common share from continuing operations
      (3) Net assets at year-end
      (4) Changes in the current cost amounts, net of inflation, of inventory and plant, property, and equipment
   d. Other information:
      (1) Purchasing power gain or loss on net monetary items
      (2) Cash dividends declared per share
      (3) Market price per common share at fiscal year-end

Format for Disclosure

The required disclosures may be displayed in several ways and may range from the minimum required disclosures to complete financial statements using the two measurement bases. If net asset figures for the five-year summary are computed from complete financial statements, this fact should be disclosed in a note to the summary. Financial reports should also explain the supplemental information presented and discuss its significance to the firm.

Suggested methods of displaying the income statement effects of changing prices are (1) the reconcilation format or (2) the statement format.

The reconcilation format is as follows:*

Income from continuing operations, as reported in the income statement		$ 9,000
Adjustments to restate costs for the effect of general inflation		
Cost of goods sold	(7,384)	
Depreciation and amortization expense	(4,130)	(11,514)
Loss from continuing operations adjusted for general inflation		(2,514)
Adjustments to reflect the difference between general inflation and changes in specific prices (current costs)		
Cost of goods sold	(1,024)	
Depreciation and amortization expense	(5,370)	(6,394)
Loss from continuing operations adjusted for changes in specific prices		$(8,908)
Gain from decline in purchasing power of net amounts owed		$ 7,729
Increase in specific prices (current cost) of inventories and property, plant, and equipment held during the year		$ 24,608
Effect of increase in general price level		18,959
Excess of increase in specific prices over increase in the general price level		$ 5,649

*This format and the statement format that follows are from the *Statement of Financial Accounting Standards No. 33*, Financial Accounting Standards Board, 1979, pp. 32–33. Copyright by the Financial Accounting Standards Board, High Ridge Park, Stamford, Connecticut 06905 U.S.A. Reprinted with permission. Copies of the complete document are available from the FASB.

The statement format is as follows:

	As Reported in the Primary Statements	Adjusted for General Inflation	Adjusted for Changes in Specific Prices (Current Costs)
Net sales and other operating revenues	$253,000	$253,000	$253,000
Cost of goods sold	197,000	204,384	205,408
Depreciation and amortization expense	10,000	14,130	19,500
Other operating expense	20,835	20,835	20,835
Interest expense	7,165	7,165	7,165
Provision for income taxes	9,000	9,000	9,000
	244,000	255,514	261,908
Income (loss) from continuing operations	$ 9,000	$(2,514)	$(8,908)
Gain from decline in purchasing power of net amounts owed		$ 7,729	$ 7,729
Increase in specific prices (current cost) of inventories and property, plant, and equipment held during the year			$ 24,608
Effect of increase in general price level			18,959
Excess of increase in specific prices over increase in the general price level			$ 5,649

Measurements

When only the minimum requirements are presented, constant dollar calculations shall be determined at the average price level for the year using the Consumer Price Index for All Urban Consumers (Appendix F of the statement). If a firm elects to present complete supplementary financial statements, the constant dollar calculations may be at either the average price level for the year or the year-end price level.

Calculations for constant dollar amounts are to be made as follows:

$$\text{Historical cost} \times \frac{\text{average index}}{\text{acquisition date index}} = \text{constant dollar cost}$$

Limitation: The upper limit for both constant dollar and current cost data is the recoverable amount for the asset. If it is necessary to reduce inventory and/or plant, property, and equipment to lower recoverable amounts, the amount of the reduction shall be figured into income from continuing operations. (This parallels lower of cost or market in conventional GAAP.)

Current cost information may be developed in any or all of several ways. Two categories of methods are mentioned in the statement: indexation and direct pricing. The FASB expects firms to experiment to find the most efficient way to arrive at current costs.

Purchasing Power Gain or Loss

The disclosures of constant dollar information require the calculation and disclosure of the purchasing power gain or loss which results from maintaining a net monetary asset position (loss) or net monetary liability position (gain) during a period of inflation. The definition of monetary items is generally cash or claims to receive or pay cash that is fixed or presently determinable without reference to some future price. Appendix D to the statement is a fairly complete listing of accounts classified as monetary or nonmonetary.

The gain or loss is determined by:

1. Determining the net monetary position at the beginning of the year from the historical cost balance sheet and adjusting this figure to the average price level for the year
2. Adding the change in the monetary position for the year (assumed to be at average prices)
3. Subtracting the net monetary position at the end of the year adjusted to the average price level for the year

For example, assume that the price level was 100 at January 1, 106 at the average for the year, and 114 at December 31.

	Historical Cost		Constant $
Net monetary assets, January 1	$100,000	$\times \frac{106}{100}$	106,000
Increase in monetary assets	9,000		9,000
			115,000
Net monetary assets, December 31	$109,000	$\times \frac{106}{114}$	101,351
Purchasing power loss			13,649

Change in Current Cost

The disclosures of current cost information require the calculation and disclosure of the change in current costs over the year net of inflation. This change is to be aggregated for both inventory and plant, property, and equipment. To arrive at the figures, separate amounts must be determined for each of these two categories. Both inventories and plant, property, and equipment use the same model to convert current cost amounts to current cost/constant dollar amounts. The difference between the change in the asset account in current dollars and the change in the asset in current cost/constant dollars is defined as the inflation component.

For example, with the same indices as above, for either inventory or plant, property, and equipment (i.e., "asset"):

	Current Cost		Current Cost/ Constant $
"Asset" balance, January 1	$100,000	$\times \dfrac{106}{100}$	106,000
Add increases (assumed at average)	15,000		15,000
Deduct decreases (assumed at average)	(8,000)		(8,000)
	107,000		113,000
Less "asset" balance, December 31	121,000	$\times \dfrac{106}{114}$	112,509
Increase/(decrease) in current cost of "asset"	$ 14,000		(491)

The inflation component in this example is $14,491.

FASB Statement 39

This Statement was issued to supplement FASB 33 by requiring current cost disclosures of mineral resource assets which originally were exempted. Therefore, firms with mineral resource assets shall include these assets at current cost or lower recoverable amount when reporting the income and asset figures on a current cost basis.

The following additional disclosures are required by firms with mineral resources other than oil and gas for each of the past five years:

1. Quantities of proved and probable resources broken down by products for joint-product resources
2. Quantities of each mineral produced
3. Quantities of reserves purchased and sold
4. Average market price for each mineral.

FASB Statement 40

FASB 33 originally permitted timberlands, growing timber, and harvested timber to be included in current cost disclosures on an adjusted historical cost basis with adjustments made by either specific or general price indices.

This supplemental Statement permits continued use of the adjusted historical cost basis or adoption of a current cost or lower recoverable amount basis to measure timber assets included in current cost information.

FASB Statement 41

Income-producing property is defined as property that is being operated under a long-term lease where cash flows from the lease are estimable and ancillary services are not a major part of the lease agreement.

FASB 33 originally permitted income-producing real estate to be included in current cost disclosures on an adjusted historical basis with adjustments made by either specific or general price indices.

This supplemental Statement permits continued use of the adjusted historical cost basis or adoption of a current cost or lower recoverable amount basis to measure income-producing real estate included in current cost information.

FASB Statement 46

This Statement relaxes the requirement for current cost information of motion picture films. Information on a current cost basis may include measurements of motion picture films on either

1. An historical cost/constant dollar basis, or
2. A current cost or lower recoverable amount basis.

FASB Statement 54

This Statement exempts investment companies, as defined in Section 3 of the Investment Company Act of 1940 (as amended), from the requirements of FASB 33.

Sources for this topic in FASB *Accounting Standards: Current Text*:
FASB Statement 47

PROFILE:

- This Statement specifies disclosure requirements for unconditional purchase obligations which meet each of three characteristics. Required disclosures depend on whether or not the obligation is recognized on the purchaser's balance sheet. The Statement does not contain criteria for determining when accounting recognition of the obligations is appropriate.

- Disclosures are also required for other long-term debt and redeemable capital stock.

This Statement specifies disclosure requirements for certain unconditional purchase obligations which are defined as obligations to transfer funds, product, or services in fixed or minimum amounts. Disclosure requirements are spelled out in this Statement for unconditional purchase obligations which have all three of the following attributes. The obligation:

1. Is noncancelable or is cancelable only upon a remote contingency, permission of the obligee, replacement of the agreement, or payment of a prohibitive penalty
2. Was part of a financing arrangement for the facilities that will produce the goods or services or for the costs of the goods or services
3. Has a term of more than one year remaining

Unconditional purchase obligations meeting the criteria above and which are *not* recognized on the purchaser's balance sheet shall be disclosed by presentation of the following information:

1. The nature and period of the obligation
2. As of the latest balance sheet date, the total fixed portion of the obligation and comparable amounts for each of the next five years
3. A description of any variable portion of the obligation
4. Total purchases under the obligation for each period an income statement is presented

It is preferable, but not mandatory, to report the amounts listed above at present value. The discount rate shall be that rate used to finance the facility providing the goods or services, if known, or the purchaser's incremental borrowing rate at the date of the obligation.

The following disclosures are required for all other obligations for each of the succeeding five years subsequent to the latest balance sheet date:

1. Total payments on unconditional purchase obligations meeting the criteria above but which have been recognized on the purchaser's balance sheet
2. Total maturities and sinking-fund payments on long-term debt
3. Total amounts required for redemption of capital stock

Sources for this topic in FASB *Accounting Standards: Current Text*:
    APB Opinion 12, Pars. 6, 7

PROFILE:

- Deferred compensation contracts that are not equivalent to pension plans require regular accrual, over the period of employment, of the estimated amounts to be paid. The accrued liability at the end of the period of employment must equal the present value of the obligation at that date.

Sources for this topic in FASB *Accounting Standards: Current Text*:

FASB Statement 43

PROFILE:

- A liability must be accrued for the cost of future absences if each of four specific criteria is met (see the text).

DISCLOSURE:

- If the liability cannot be estimated, this fact must be disclosed.
- Accounting changes shall be applied retroactively by restatement, with disclosure of the effect on each year's income and per share amounts.

A liability must be accrued for the cost of employees' future absences if all four of the following criteria are met:

1. The cost relates to past service of the employees.
2. The employees' rights to the compensation are vested or may be carried forward.
3. It is probable that payment will be made.
4. The cost may be reasonably estimated.

If a liability is not accrued only because a reasonable estimate of the cost cannot be made, this fact must be disclosed. Employers are not required to accrue sick pay which is not vested, even though benefits may be carried forward to future periods.

Accounting changes caused by application of this Statement must be made by retroactive restatement of prior financial statements as far as is practicable. Where all affected years are not restated, the cumulative effect on years not restated shall be reported in income of the earliest year reported. The effect of the restatement on income before extraordinary items, net income, and related per share amounts shall be disclosed for all years restated in the period this Statement is first applied.

Sources for this topic in FASB *Accounting Standards: Current Text*:

ARB 43, Chap. 13B

APB Opinion 25

FASB Interpretation 28

PROFILE:

- Compensation is generally not involved in plans where a broad offering is made to all employees nor in more restricted offers where the incentive to purchase is not larger than would be necessary to entice all shareholders to buy shares.
- For compensatory plans:

1. Compensation is measured at the date of the grant.

2. Compensation is the excess of market value of the stock over the option price.

3. Compensation expense should be distributed to the periods benefited by the contract.

DISCLOSURE:

- At balance sheet date: number of shares at option, the option price, and the number of shares exercisable
- For the year: number of shares issued and the option price

Requirements for Noncompensatory Plans

1. The plan must be offered to all full-time employees except that those not meeting certain employment qualifications, officers, and employees owning more than a specified amount of stock may be excluded.
2. The plan offers the stock uniformly in either absolute terms or as a percentage of compensation.
3. The time period for purchase or exercise is reasonable and limited.
4. The price discount for the shares is not excessive.

Compensatory Plans

If all four of the qualities above are not present, a plan is classified as compensatory even though compensation expense recognition may not be required. This opinion reaffirmed the ARB 43 position that compensation is measured at the date of the grant, but the opinion elaborated on the definition of this measurement date as the date when both the number of shares and the price are known. In reaffirming the ARB 43 position, this opinion also restricted the measurement amount to the quoted market price of the stock or an estimate if such price is unavailable.

Applying the Measurement Principle to Special Situations

1. The cost of treasury shares generally is not to be used to measure compensation. An exception is made for plans meeting the requirements of item 3 below *and* such treasury shares were reacquired during the period and awarded shortly after the end of the period.
2. The measurement date is not changed by a provision that the number of shares issuable to an employee is reduced upon termination.
3. The measurement date may be the end of a fiscal period rather than the award date if such an award is part of a formal plan which

indicates the factors upon which the award is based and that basis is service in the current period.

4. Renewal or extension of a plan establishes a new measurement date.

5. Transfer of assets or stock to third parties under terms of the plan will not affect the measurement date unless such transfer is unequivocally for the benefit of the grantee under the original terms of the grant.

6. The measurement date for a convertible stock award is the date when the conversion rate becomes known. Compensation should be measured by the larger market value of the stock or other security into which the stock may be converted.

7. Cash paid to a grantee in settlement or to repurchase shares recently issued under the plan shall be used to measure compensation. This does not include cash paid to taxing authorities from proceeds of the sale of grantees' shares to cover withholding taxes.

Accounting for Compensation

Compensation cost (market price minus option price) should be charged to one or more periods in which the issuing corporation receives services, and this cost shall be recorded as partial consideration for the shares issued. The period for which the corporation receives services may be specified by the plan or inferred from past awards.

When shares are issued several periods subsequent to an award, the issuing corporation should accrue compensation for each period covered by the award based on the market price of the shares at the end of each period. When shares are issued before all services are received, the unearned compensation must be reported as a contra item in stockholders' equity.

Adjustments such as those due to forfeiture must be treated in the period of forfeiture by adjusting compensation expense.

Income tax expense must not be reduced by more than the tax effect of compensation expense related to the plan. Tax deductions taken in periods different from accounting recognition of compensation are timing differences requiring deferred tax accounting.

Reimbursements to employees for their expenses related to the plan must be charged against income.

Interpretation 28

Plans involving stock appreciation rights and other variable plan awards are covered by APB Opinion 25. Several clarifications regarding these plans are:

1. If the grant is for past services, compensation shall be charged to expense in the year of the grant.

2. Compensation shall be adjusted prior to the measurement date for changes in the market value of the stock by adjusting the compensation expense of the period in which the stock price changes.

3. When an employee has several choices under a variable plan, compensation shall be determined on the basis of the election the employee is most likely to make.

It is to be presumed that an employee will elect to exercise stock appreciation rights and compensation shall be accrued accordingly. If the employee subsequently elects the stock option, accrued compensation is deemed consideration for the stock issued. If the employee forfeits his or her rights, the accrued compensation shall be offset to compensation expense for the period.

4. Stock appreciation rights and other variable plan awards, to the extent payable in stock, are common stock equivalents for earnings per share purposes.

Sources for this topic in FASB *Accounting Standards: Current Text*:

ARB 43, Chap. 12; ARB 51

FASB Statement 13

PROFILE:

- Control is a necessary, but not sufficient condition for consolidation. Usefulness of resulting statements is the criterion for consolidation.

- Intercompany profits and losses should be eliminated in full.

- In preparing an income statement it is preferable to include complete subsidiary operations and subtract the total preacquisition income. For a disposition it is preferable to omit complete subsidiary operations and add the total predisposition income.

- The equity method generally should be used for unconsolidated subsidiaries.

- Many detailed disclosures are required when the cost method is used for unconsolidated subsidiaries.

When to Consolidate

The decision to consolidate is somewhat subjective. A necessary prerequisite is at least a 50% interest in the outstanding voting shares, but consolidation should not be made when control is not present (e.g., in bankruptcy) or is temporary. The decision to consolidate should be made from the perspective of the most useful presentation. In some circumstances it would be better to issue separate statements for a subsidiary rather than to consolidate it (e.g., bank, insurance, or finance subsidiaries of a manufacturing parent company).

Reporting Periods

Reports for subsidiaries' fiscal periods that end within three months of the parent's fiscal year end may be consolidated, but material events occurring between the fiscal period ending dates must be disclosed.

Intercompany Transactions

Intercompany profits or losses on assets held by a constituent to the consolidation must be eliminated and any taxes paid on these profits must be deferred. The total profit or loss must be eliminated even though a minority interest exists.

Elimination of Intercompany Investments

Retained earnings or deficit of a purchased subsidiary that existed prior to acquisition must not be included in consolidated retained earnings.

Shares of the parent owned by the subsidiary must not be reported as outstanding shares in the consolidated balance sheet.

Piecemeal Acquisition

When substantial blocks of subsidiary stock are acquired at different times, retained earnings at acquisition must be established separately for each block of shares. This may be delayed if many small acquisitions of stock are followed by a major purchase in which control is achieved. In this case the final purchase may be used for the effective acquisition date.

Earnings in Year of Acquisition or Disposal

In the year of acquisition it is preferable to consolidate the complete income statement of the subsidiary and deduct preacquisition earnings. Alternatively, it is permissible to consolidate revenues and expenses of the subsidiary since the date of acquisition.

For disposals, it is preferable not to consolidate the income statement of the disposed subsidiary but instead to include the pre-disposition earnings as a single figure in the consolidated income statement.

Unconsolidated Subsidiaries

The equity method must be used to account for unconsolidated subsidiaries unless control does not rest with the parent, control is temporary, or because of uncertainties of a foreign subsidiary. In the latter cases the cost method must be used and provision must be made for impairment of the investment. Disclosures required for the cost method include:

1. Cost of the investment.
2. Equity in net assets.
3. Dividends received by the parent.
4. Equity in earnings for the period.
5. Amortization of difference between cost and equity in assets.
6. Intercompany gains and losses.
7. If subsidiaries reported by the cost method in total are material in relation to the consolidated financial position or operating results, either separate statements or a summary of assets, liabilities, and earnings must be reported.

Sources for this topic in FASB *Accounting Standards: Current Text*:
    FASB Statements 5, 11, 38
    FASB Interpretations 14, 34

PROFILE:

- FASB 5 classifies contingencies as probable, possible, and remote. Generally, accrual is required only for probable losses, while disclosure is required for possible losses, and no mention need be made of remotely possible loss contingencies. Specific disclosures are required for probable and possible loss contingencies.

- FASB 11 deals with accounting for accounting changes required by adoption of FASB 5. Essentially, adoption of FASB 5 is a change in accounting principle requiring cumulative effect adjustment, including restatement of prior periods if such earlier statements are reissued for comparative purposes.

DISCLOSURE:

- See the details in the text for each type of contingency.

FASB Statement 5

Loss contingencies must be charged to income if *both* of the following conditions are present:

1. It is probable that the loss has occurred (future events will confirm the supposition of loss).
2. The amount of the loss can be estimated with reasonable accuracy.

Disclosure of the provision for such loss and the amount may be necessary for adequate disclosure. Disclosure shall also be made if both conditions are not met (i.e., accrual is inappropriate) but there is a possibility that a loss has occurred. In this case disclosure should include a description of the contingency and the amount or range of possible loss or a statement that an estimate cannot be made.

Disclosure may be necessary of possible and/or probable losses which did not exist at the date of the financial statements but which occur before such statements are issued. If the financial statements would be misleading without disclosure, information must be disclosed regarding the nature of the loss or loss contingency, including the amount, range of the amount, or a statement that the amount cannot be estimated.

Remote loss contingencies must be disclosed if they are guarantees of indebtedness or receivables or obligations to grant credit. The disclosure must indicate a description of the guarantee and amounts thereof.

Interpretation 14

When it is probable that a loss has occurred and the amount is only reasonably estimable within a range, some specific amount must be accrued. The amount accrued should be the best estimate within the range or, if not practical, the minimum of the range.

Interpretation 34

"Guarantees of indebtedness," as this term is used in FASB 5, is interpreted to include *indirect* guarantees of indebtedness of others.

FASB Statement 11

Since FASB 5 eliminated the accrual of reserves for general contingencies that do not meet the two new criteria for loss accrual, a question arises as to how the change in accounting principle should be treated.

Financial statements for periods beginning prior to July 1, 1975, reissued for comparative purposes, must be restated to conform with FASB 5. The cumulative effect of the change on retained earnings at the beginning of the earliest year presented shall be used in determining income of that earliest period. In the year this restatement is first made, the financial statements shall describe the restatement and display its effect on income before extraordinary items, net income, and per share amounts for all periods restated.

If it is not practicable to determine amounts for restatement of any periods to be presented, the cumulative effect of the change must be included in income of the period in which FASB Statement 5 is first applied.

Sources for this topic in FASB *Accounting Standards: Current Text*:
APB Opinion 14

PROFILE:

- Convertible debt: No portion of the proceeds from the sale of convertible debt shall be attributed to the conversion feature.
- Debt with detachable warrants: the proceeds of issuance shall be prorated between debt and equity in proportion to the fair values of the two elements at time of issuance.

Sources for this topic in FASB *Accounting Standards: Current Text*:

APB Opinion 26

FASB Statement 4

FASB Technical Bulletin 80–1

PROFILE:

- All extinguishments of debt, including convertible debt, are essentially alike and the accounting for all extinguishments must be the same without consideration of the means used to retire the debt.

- The difference between book value of the debt and price to reacquire the debt instruments must be recognized in income as a gain or loss in the period the transaction occurred.

- Gains and losses from extinguishment of all debt shall be combined. If the total is material, the gain or loss should be reported as an extraordinary item, net of tax. This requirement applies regardless of whether the extinguishment is early, late, or at the scheduled retirement date. Exempted are gains and losses from cash acquisitions of debt to satisfy sinking-fund requirements.

DISCLOSURE:

- Gain or loss from extinguishment must be reported separately,

- If gains and losses are classified extraordinary, disclosure should include the following:

1. A description of the transactions and identification of sources of funds used, if practicable

2. The income tax effect of the extinguishment

3. The per share gain or loss net of tax

Sources for this topic in FASB *Accounting Standards: Current Text*:

FASB Statement 49

PROFILE:

- This Statement deals with transactions covering the sale and repurchase (for financing purposes) of product and provides standards for accounting by the seller/purchaser. Criteria are provided to identify qualifying transactions and standards are established for variations in financing arrangements.

DISCLOSURE:

- No special requirements

This Statement applies to product financing arrangements wherein the original purchaser or producer of the product (called the sponsor of the financing arrangement) sells such product to another party and simultaneously agrees to repurchase the same or equivalent product. The Statement also applies if the sponsor arranges for the other party to purchase the product from suppliers and then agrees to purchase the product from the other party.

Specifically, the Statement applies to product financing arrangements that meet *both* of the following conditions:

1. The financing arrangement provides for reacquisition of the product by the sponsor at fixed prices. This condition is met if *any one* of the following exists:

   a. The fixed price is a guarantee of resale prices to third parties.

   b. The sponsor is not legally bound to reacquire the product but an option price is so attractive as to make repurchase economically compelling.

   c. The sponsor is not legally bound to reacquire the product but the other party has an option that can force the reacquisition.

2. The payments to the other party are established in the agreement and the amounts will be adjusted for fluctuations in purchase and holding costs of the other party.

The sponsor shall account for qualifying product financing arrangements as follows:

1. If the sponsor sold the product to the other party:

   a. A liability shall be recorded upon receipt of the proceeds from the other party.

   b. The product shall not be recorded as a sale.

   c. The product shall be reflected on the sponsor's balance sheet.

2. If the other party purchased the product from a supplier:

   a. The product shall be recorded as an asset.

   b. A liability shall be recorded when the other party purchases the product.

3. Costs incurred in excess of original purchase or production cost are financing and holding costs and shall be accounted for as the sponsor would properly account for these costs in the absence of a product financing arrangement.

Sources for this topic in FASB *Accounting Standards: Current Text*:

FASB Statement 15

FASB Technical Bulletins 79-6, 7; 80-2; 81-6

PROFILE:

- Troubled debt restructuring exists when a creditor grants a concession to a debtor that it otherwise would not consider. Accounting for TDR's varies by classification of:
  1. Transfer of assets or equity
  2. Modification of terms
  3. Combination of types
- Debtors take gains on restructuring and gains or losses on transfer of assets.
- Creditors take losses on restructuring if the value of the asset received or the total of future receipts is less than the book value of the receivable.

DISCLOSURE:

- Both debtor and creditor are required to make detailed disclosures following a TDR; see the text following.

Satisfaction of a debt is a troubled debt restructuring (TDR) only when the creditor grants a concession to the debtor. In these circumstances the debtor will realize a gain if the debt is fully satisfied and the creditor will realize a loss. For partially settled debts, gains and losses may or may not be recognized, depending on how extensive the concession by the creditor is.

Accounting for TDRs by Debtors

Transfer of Assets in Full Settlement: The debtor shall recognize a gain on restructuring measured by the difference between the fair value of the asset surrendered and the carrying value of the debt. The debtor shall also recognize a gain or loss on the transfer of assets measured by the difference between the fair value of the asset transferred and its carrying value.

Grant of Equity Interest in Full Settlement: The debtor shall recognize a gain on restructuring measured by the difference between the fair value of its equity securities issued and the carrying value of the debt.

Modification of Terms: When a TDR involves a change of terms for payment of the debt (e.g., reduction of principal and/or reduction of interest rate) the debtor generally shall account for the improved terms prospectively. Prospective accounting requires calculation of a new effective interest rate which equates the new future cash payments with the book value of the debt. Interest expense in future periods will be calculated with this new effective rate. If the absolute amount of the revised cash payments (principal + interest) is less than the book value of the debt, the debtor shall recognize a gain on restructuring to the extent of this difference. This will result in reduction of the carrying value of the debt to the sum of the future payments and future periods will not report interest expense.

Combination of Types: When assets are transferred *and* terms are modified, the following sequence shall be followed: First, the debt shall be reduced by the fair value of the asset or equity transferred (with appropriate gain or loss on asset transfer). Second, the modification of terms methods shall be applied with gain on restructuring recognized only if the absolute sum of future cash outlays is less than the remaining book value of debt.

If aggregate gains from restructuring are material, they shall be reported as extraordinary items. Where future interest payments will fluctuate, TDR calculations shall be based on rates existing at the restructuring date and future fluctuations shall be treated as changes in estimates. Legal fees and other direct costs incurred for a TDR shall be allocated to reduce the proceeds from issue of stock (if applicable) and to reduce the gain from restructuring. If no gain is recognized, these costs shall be expensed.

Disclosure: Disclosure for a restructuring shall include:

1. Changes in terms or features of settlement
2. Total gain on restructuring and the tax effect
3. Total net gain or loss on transfer of assets for TDRs
4. Per share amount, net of tax, of gain on restructuring

For periods after the TDR, disclosure shall indicate the amounts of contingent payments included in the restructured debt. If further amounts of contingent payments which are not included in the balance of restructured debt meet the requirements of FASB 5, they shall be disclosed with an indication of the conditions under which they will be paid or forgiven.

Accounting for TDRs by Creditors

Receipt of Assets in Full Settlement: The creditor shall recognize a loss measured by the difference between the fair value of the asset and the carrying value of the receivable.

Modification of Terms: When no assets are received on the restructuring and only the terms of the receivable are changed, the creditor shall account for the restructuring prospectively and not reduce the value of the receivable. Prospective accounting involves calculation of a new effective interest rate which equates the book value of the receivable with the new expected cash receipts. This rate then shall be used to record future interest income. If total future cash receipts (principal + interest) is less than the book value of the receivable, the creditor shall recognize a loss and write the receivable down to the sum of such future receipts. In this circumstance future collections will be recovery of the receivable and no interest income will be recorded.

Combination of Types: When the restructuring includes both receipt of assets and modification of terms, the fair value of assets received shall first reduce the receivable and then the methods for modification of terms shall be applied.

Creditors' losses shall be reported in accordance with provisions of APBO 30. If losses have previously been provided for with an allowance for bad debts, this allowance shall absorb the reduction in the receivable and a TDR loss should not be recorded. If future receipts are expected to fluctuate from changing interest rates, TDR calculations shall be based on the interest rate existing at the date of the TDR. Future changes in the rates shall be treated as changes in accounting estimates unless use of that rate results in a further erosion in the present value of the restructured receivable. In these circumstances the receivable shall be reduced to the new present value and a loss recorded. Legal fees for a TDR shall be expensed in the period incurred.

Disclosure: Statements or notes shall include information as follows:

1. For remaining restructured receivables:
   a. Total investment
   b. Pro forma interest income that would have been received if TDR had not occurred
   c. Interest income that was recorded for the period on those receivables
2. Commitments for loans of additional funds to debtors for which a TDR was recorded

Sources for this topic in FASB *Accounting Standards: Current Text*:
>   ARB 43, Chap. 9A, 9C; ARB 44
>   APB Opinions 1, 6, 12

PROFILE:
- The text on the following pages deal with the topics of:
  1. Depreciation guideline lives
  2. Declining-balance depreciation
  3. Depreciation and high costs
  4. Depreciation on appreciation
  5. Depreciation of emergency facilities

DISCLOSURE:
- The following disclosures should be made in financial statements or footnotes:
  1. Depreciation expense
  2. Amounts of major categories of depreciable assets at the balance sheet date
  3. Accumulated depreciation at the balance sheet date by major category in item 2 or in total
  4. Description of depreciation methods used for the major categories

Depreciation Guideline Lives

Useful lives of depreciable property for accounting must be brought into agreement with IRS Guideline lives to the extent that Guideline lives are reasonable for the entity.

Provision for deferred taxes must be made when Guideline lives are shorter than lives used for accounting.

When regulators will not allow provision for deferred taxes related to adoption of Guideline lives, such provision may be omitted but disclosure of such omission is required.

Declining-balance Depreciation

Declining-balance depreciation, including the sum-of-the-years'-digits method, are acceptable methods for depreciation.

When a change is made to a declining-balance method, the rules of APB Opinion 20, *Accounting Changes*, apply.

When declining-balance methods are used for tax purposes and other methods are used for accounting, deferred tax accounting is required.

Depreciation and High Costs

Recorded depreciation must be based on the cost and useful life of assets regardless of inflation.

It is within the province of management to make appropriations of retained earnings or otherwise disclose the problem of the need to retain earned income to replace productive facilities at higher price levels.

Depreciation on Appreciation

Property, plant, and equipment must not be written up for changing market values of these assets.

Exceptions to the write-up prohibition are quasi-reorganizations and certain foreign operations. When appreciation has been recorded, depreciation must be calculated on the higher basis.

Depreciation of Emergency Facilities

For accounting purposes the depreciable life of emergency facilities covered by certificates of necessity must be determined as if no such certificate existed. Thus, when depreciation allowed for tax purposes by virtue of the certificate of necessity is materially higher than accounting depreciation otherwise would be, the smaller depreciation figure must be used in the accounts.

Sources for this topic in FASB *Accounting Standards: Current Text*:

    APB Opinions 15, 30

    FASB Statements 21, 55

    FASB Interpretations 28, 31

    FASB Technical Bulletin 79–8

PROFILE:

- All income statements require display of EPS:*

  1. Simple equity structures require only single EPS figures.

  2. Complex equity structures require primary and fully diluted EPS figures.

- EPS figures should be presented for income before extraordinary items and for net income.

DISCLOSURE:

- EPS figures should be prominently displayed on the face of the income statement. Supplemental additional disclosures are sometimes required; see the text following.

---

*Not required of nonpublic companies.

Earnings per share figures are required on all income statements* and EPS should be shown for income before extraordinary items and for net income. See Sec. A06 for variations in presentation when accounting changes and correction of errors occur. When earnings of a prior period which is presented have been restated because of accounting recognition of a prior period adjustment, the earnings per share figures for that period should also be restated. When dual EPS figures are required for any one period which is presented among several others, dual EPS figures should be presented for all periods.

Simple capital structures containing only common stock or which have, in addition, no potentially dilutive securities are required to present only one set of figures. As a practical matter, a 3% test is used to measure the extent of dilution for relatively simple capital structures. If the potential dilution would result in less than a 3% reduction in EPS, the dilution can be ignored.

Complex capital structures require presentation of primary (P-EPS) and fully diluted (FD-EPS) earnings per share figures to be displayed with equal prominence.

Additional Disclosures for Complex Capital Structures

Financial statements should include an explanation of the rights and privileges of the several securities a firm has issued.

A statement should indicate the basis used to calculate both P-EPS and FD-EPS, identification of issues deemed to be common stock equivalents, and an indication of those issues which have been included in the FD-EPS.

Supplementary EPS figures should be presented in a note when conversions have occurred during the current period and the resulting EPS figures are different than they would have been if these conversions had occurred at the beginning of the period. If conversion occurred between the end of the period and issue of the financial statements, similar supplementary EPS figures should be presented. If common stock has been sold to retire preferred stock or debt during or after the current period, supplementary EPS figures should be presented to show EPS as if the transaction had occurred as of the beginning of the current period.

*Not required of nonpublic companies.

Calculation and Display of EPS

Following are examples, taken from APB Opinion 15, of the income statement display of EPS for both simple equity structures and complex equity structures. These EPS designations are recommended by APB Opinion 15, although the EPS for the extraordinary item is not required. Note that the terms "primary EPS" and "fully diluted EPS" are not used in the disclosures; they are for reference convenience.

EXAMPLE OF DISCLOSURE OF EARNINGS PER SHARE
Simple Capital Structure*

	Thousands (Except per share data)	
Bottom of Income Statement	1968	1967
Income before extraordinary item	$ 9,150	$7,650
Extraordinary item—gain on sale of property less applicable income taxes	900	—
Net income	$10,050	$7,650
Earnings per common share		
Income before extraordinary item	$ 2.77	$ 2.32
Extraordinary item	$ 0.28	—
Net income	$ 3.05	$ 2.32

Complex Capital Structure

	Thousands (Except per share data)	
Bottom of Income Statement	1968	1967
Income before extraordinary item	$12,900	$10,300
Extraordinary item—gain on sale of property less applicable income taxes	900	—
Net income	$13,800	$10,300

*This example and the one that follows come from *APB Opinion 15, Earnings per Share*, copyright 1969 by the American Institute of Certified Public Accountants, Inc. Used with permission.

	Thousands (Except per share data)	
Bottom of Income Statement	*1968*	*1967*
Earnings per common share and common equivalent share (Note X)		
Income before extraordinary item	$ 3.20	$ 2.75
Extraordinary item	$ 0.22	—
Net income	$ 3.42	$ 2.75
Earnings per common share—assuming full dilution (Note X)		
Income before extraordinary item	$ 3.11	$ 2.66
Extraordinary item	$ 0.21	—
Net income	$ 3.32	$ 2.66

Simple Equity Structure EPS

$$\text{EPS} = \frac{\text{appropriate income number}^*}{\text{weighted average shares outstanding}}$$

*Income before extraordinary items or net income.

Complex Equity Structure EPS

Primary EPS:

$$\text{EPS} = \frac{\text{income number}^* \ (-\text{ preferred div.})^\dagger \ (+\text{ bond interest})^\ddagger}{\text{wtd. avg. shares} + \text{common stock equivalent shares}}$$

*Income before extraordinary items or net income.

†Preferred dividends should be subtracted when either nonconvertible or convertible but not CSE *and* the issue is cumulative (regardless of dividend declaration) or noncumulative but dividends were declared.

‡If bonds are CSE, after-tax interest should be added.

Fully Diluted EPS:

$$EPS = \frac{\text{income number* (– preferred div.)}^\dagger \text{ (+ bond interest)}^\ddagger}{\text{wtd. avg. shares + CSE shares}^\S + \text{"if converted" shares}^\P}$$

*Income before extraordinary items or net income.

$\dagger$Preferred dividends should be subtracted for nonconvertible issues that are either cumulative or noncumulative when dividends have been declared.

$\ddagger$Bond interest after tax should be added for convertible bonds.

$\S$CSE shares for options and warrants may be higher than that used for P-EPS if market price is higher than the average—see the treasury stock method below.

$\P$Number of shares that preferred or bonds are convertible into.

Common Stock Equivalent Shares

Certain issues of securities may be considered the equivalent of common stock for purposes of calculating P-EPS. Convertible preferred stock and convertible bonds are candidates for CSE status. These securities shall be designated CSE if, at the time they were originally issued, their cash yield was less than two-thirds of the then-current average Aa corporate bond yield.

Options and warrants are always considered CSE, but inclusion in P-EPS calculation depends on potential dilution as measured by the difference between the market price and the option price of the shares. The *treasury stock method* is used to calculate the number of CSE shares. The number of CSE shares is the number of shares issuable in excess of those that could be purchased with the proceeds of exercise of the options. A formula for the calculation is:

$$\text{CSE shares (for options and warrants)} = \text{shares at option} \times \frac{\text{average market price} - \text{option price}}{\text{avg. mkt. price}}$$

This calculation is required only when the average market price is greater than the option price. If, at year-end, the market price is greater than the average price, CSE shares for FD-EPS should be calculated using the larger year-end price, which will yield a larger dilution.

If application of this treasury stock method results in a number of CSE shares which is larger than 20% of the outstanding shares at year-end, the treasury stock method should be modified. In these circumstances assumed proceeds from exercise of options in excess of that required to repurchase 20% of the year-end shares should be used to reduce debt and, if necessary, acquire U.S. government securities or commercial paper on a pro forma basis. Application of this technique requires pro forma adjustment to the earnings used for EPS calculations.

Participating securities and two-class common stocks are also CSE if they share in earnings the same as common stock. Contingent shares are also CSE if they are to be issued on the passage of time and no consideration will be received on their issuance.

No Antidilution

It is very important that all adjustments and calculations do not result in an increase in EPS. This is referred to as antidilution. Each adjustment to the numerator and denominator should be made with and without the item in question to make sure that EPS does not increase.

Interpretation 31

In applying the treasury stock method, the proceeds of the exercise of the options is defined as the sum of:

1. The employee's payment
2. Measurable compensation for future services (not past services) not yet expensed
3. Windfall tax benefits of the compensation deduction

Sources for this topic in FASB *Accounting Standards: Current Text:*
   APB Opinion 19

PROFILE:
- A Statement of Changes in Financial Position is required as a basic financial statement.
- The Statement should use the broad "all financial resources" approach but may be prepared with either cash or working capital as the definition of funds.

DISCLOSURE:
- No special disclosures required beyond those of the statement itself

A Statement of Changes in Financial Position is required for all periods for which an income statement is issued. The statement shall use the "all financial resources" approach so as to report all major financing and investing transactions.

The statement may use the cash or working capital basis for funds provided (or used) by operations. If the working capital basis is used, a list of the changes in each element of working capital is required as a supplement to the statement.

Considerable flexibility is permitted in the format of the statement. The statement should begin with net income or loss before extraordinary items and proceed toward either cash or working capital provided (or used) by operations. Alternatively, the cash or working capital effect of revenue and expenses may be presented in arriving at funds provided (or used) by operations. Extraordinary items and their funds effect should be reported separately from normal items.

Beyond the funds effect of operations, the "all financial resources" approach requires reporting the funds effect of:

1. Acquisition and disposal of fixed assets, intangibles, and investments
2. Issuance and extinguishment of debt
3. Issuance and reacquisition of capital stock
4. Dividends
5. Conversion to common stock of preferred stock and/or bonds

Sources for this topic in FASB *Accounting Standards: Current Text*:
ARB 43, Chap. 2A

PROFILE:

- It is recommended that financial statements for one or more prior years be presented with those of the current year for comparability purposes. Original footnotes to financial statements of those prior years, if still of significance, should be repeated or referred to. Explanations should be provided for changes in classification that affect comparability between periods presented.
- Accounting changes and correction of errors, however, should be reported in accordance with Sec. A06.

DISCLOSURE:

- No special requirements

Sources for this topic in FASB *Accounting Standards: Current Text*:

FASB Statements 8, 20

FASB Interpretations 15, 17

PROFILE:

- These rules are applicable for fiscal years beginning before December 15, 1982. For Fiscal years after this date FASB 52 applies—see Sec. F60.
- This Statement sets standards for translating amounts denominated in a foreign currency:

1. Transactions initially should be recorded in dollars and cash, receivables and payables should be adjusted for current exchange rates at balance sheet dates.

2. Financial statement translations should be determined as follows:

   a. cash, receivables and payables at current exchange rates

   b. historical cost accounts at historical exchange rates

   c. accounts carried at market prices at current exchange rates.

3. Exchange gains and losses should be recorded in income of the period when the rate changes.

DISCLOSURE:

- Several requirements; see text following.

This Statement specifies standards for the translation of foreign currency transactions and foreign currency financial statements into dollars so they may be combined with an enterprise's financial statements. A major objective of the translation standard is to have resulting translations consistent with U.S. generally accepted accounting principles.

Foreign Currency Transactions

With the exception of forward exchange contracts, all foreign currency transactions are subject to the following rules:

1. Transactions shall be recorded in dollars on the transaction date using the exchange rate at that date.
2. Cash, receivables and payables denominated in a foreign currency shall be adjusted to the dollar equivalent at each balance sheet date using the exchange rate at that date.
3. Assets carried at market prices shall first be expressed in terms of the current foreign market price at each balance sheet date and then translated at the exchange rate at that date.

Foreign Financial Statements

Financial statements expressed in foreign currencies must be adjusted, if necessary, to conform with U.S. generally accepted accounting principles before the standards for foreign currency translation are applied.

The following rules apply to the translation of foreign financial statements:

1. Cash, receivables and payables shall be translated at the current exchange rate at the balance sheet date. If the foreign statements contain amounts that are also denominated in other currencies (including dollars), those amounts shall first be translated at the

current exchange rate between the foreign currency and those other currencies.

2. The translation rate for all other assets and liabilities depends on the measurement basis for those accounts. Accounts that are properly carried at historical prices shall be translated at historical exchange rates. Accounts that are carried at current or future prices shall be translated at current exchange rates.

3. Revenues and expenses should be translated to produce the same results had the transactions originally been recorded in dollars. Use of an average exchange rate for the period is acceptable for this purpose. An exception to this rule applies to revenues and expenses that are related to assets and liabilities translated at historical rates. These revenues and expenses should also be translated at the historical rate.

4. Care must be exercised in the application of the above rules to ensure that the translated statements are in conformance with U.S. generally accepted accounting principles. Two areas of particular concern are the cost-or-market inventory method and inter-period tax allocation:

   a. The test for cost-or-market, whichever is lower, should be performed on dollars after the translation (See FASB Interpretation 17 at the end of this section).

   b. Timing differences may require adjustment in dollars even though no adjustment was made in the foreign statements.

Exchange Gains and Losses

Exchange gains and losses, which result from translation of transactions and financial statements as well as conversion of foreign currencies, should be included in net income in the period that the exchange rate changes. The term "period" here includes interim periods so exchange gains and losses should be reported in the interim period in which they occur.

Income Tax Consequences of Rate Changes

Exchange gains and losses resulting in timing differences require interperiod tax allocation.

Use of historical rates for translation of revenues and expenses may create an unusual relationship between the foreign income and related income taxes. This effect of a rate change is not deemed to be a timing difference and tax allocation for the difference is inappropriate.

Forward Exchange Contracts

With one exception, gains or losses on forward exchange contracts shall be included in net income of the period in which the rate changes. Calculation of the gain or loss depends on whether the contract is a hedge or speculation. For hedges the gain or loss is determined by the difference between the exchange rates at the balance sheet date and at the inception of the contract (or previous date of gain or loss recognition). For speculative contracts the gain or loss is measured by the difference between the forward rate of the contract and the forward rate available for the remaining period of the contract.

The exception to immediate recognition of gains and losses applies to hedges of identifiable foreign currency commitments that meet all of the following conditions:

1. The forward exchange contract covers the period from the original commitment to the settlement date or later,
2. The forward exchange contract is for the same currency as the original commitment, and
3. The original commitment is not cancelable.

If all three of these conditions are met any gain or loss shall be deferred and combined with the translated amount of the related foreign currency transaction. If the hedge contract is for a larger amount than the original commitment, or for a period beyond the settlement date, gain or loss should be recognized for the portion of the contract not needed to hedge the original commitment.

Disclosure

Aggregate exchange gains or losses, including gains and losses on forward exchange contracts, included in net income should be disclosed in the financial statements or notes.

The effect of rate changes on net income, other than those included in recognized exchange gains and losses, should be described and quantified, if practicable, and the methods used to determine the effect should be described.

It may be necessary to disclose significant rate changes and their effects which occur subsequent to the date of the financial statements.

Interpretation 15

This Interpretation deals with certain questions relating to the application of FASB 8 to foreign stock life insurance companies. The Interpretation is summarized as follows:

1. Unamortized policy acquisition costs shall be translated at historical rates.
2. Computation of the loss for reserve deficiencies shall be made in dollars after the related accounts are translated.

Interpretation 17

For purposes of applying the lower of cost-or-market rule, which is required by FASB 8 to be applied to dollars after translation, the translated market price is defined as the current foreign currency replacement cost translated at the current exchange rate. The traditional ceiling and floor on market prices are interpreted to mean that translated market

1. shall not exceed net realizeable value in the foreign currency translated at the current rate, and

2. shall not be less than net realizeable value in the foreign currency less a normal profit translated at the current rate.

Sources for this topic in FASB *Accounting Standards: Current Text*:

ARB 43, Chap. 12

FASB Statement 52

PROFILE:

- This Statement supersedes FASB 8 and FASB 20 and is effective for fiscal years beginning on or after December 15, 1982.
- Foreign financial statements shall be translated from the functional currency using a current exchange rate. Balance sheet accounts are to be translated at the current rate at the date of the balance sheet and income statements accounts are to be translated at the rate of exchange at the transaction date or at a weighted average rate for the period. Translation adjustments shall be accumulated in the equity section of the reporting entity.
- Foreign currency transactions shall be recorded at a current exchange rate on the transaction date and transaction gains or losses should be included in income in the period in which the rate changes.

DISCLOSURE:

- Aggregate transaction gains or losses
- Analysis of changes in the cumulative translation adjustments

This Statement establishes new accounting and reporting standards for foreign currency transactions and for translating foreign currency financial statements which are included within the financial statements of the reporting entity. It does not set standards for general translation of foreign currency financial statements for other purposes.

Objectives of Translation

Translation of foreign currency financial statements which are to be consolidated with the reporting entity should meet the following objectives:

a. The information presented should be consistent with the expected impact of an exchange rate change on the reporting entity's equity and cash flow

b. The effect on the consolidated statements should be the results of the foreign statements measured in the functional currency and reported under U.S. generally accepted accounting principles.

The Functional Currency

Assets, liabilities and operations of a foreign entity shall be measured with the currency of the country in which the entity operates (its functional currency). If such entity has separate operations in other countries those operations might have a different functional currency. Generally, once the functional currency is determined for an entity it shall be used consistently and changed only when it is clear that the functional currency has changed. Prior financial statements should not be restated for a change in functional currency.

When records are not maintained in the functional currency, translation into the functional currency is required before financial statements are translated into the reporting currency.

When the foreign entity operates in an economy of high inflation (100% or more in 3 years), the financial statements shall be restated directly into the reporting currency.

Translation of Foreign Currency Statements

Financial statements shall be translated with a current exchange rate. The exchange rate at the balance sheet date shall be used for assets and liabilities. The exchange rate at the transaction date, or a weighted average exchange rate, shall be used for revenues, expenses, gains and losses.

Translation adjustments shall be accumulated and reported as a separate component of equity and shall not be included in income. Upon sale or substantial liquidation of a foreign entity the portion of the translation adjustment related to that entity shall be removed and reported as part of the gain or loss for the transaction.

Foreign Currency Transactions

For transactions denominated in a foreign currency, a foreign currency transaction gain or loss should be recorded in the period in which the exchange rate changes. Further, an additional gain or loss should be recorded in the period of settlement if the exchange rate changes from the previous balance sheet date. For exceptions to this rule, see the discussion of exclusions below. The effect of this standard will be achieved by:

a. recording all accounts for a foreign currency transaction in the functional currency by using the exchange rate at the transaction date, and

b. adjusting all accounts denominated in the foreign currency using the exchange rate at the balance sheet date and taking the net difference to the exchange gain or loss account.

Forward Exchange Contracts

Forward exchange contracts, including other arrangements which are substantially the same in effect, are foreign currency transactions for which gains or losses should be recorded in current income in the same manner as other foreign currency transactions. The gain or loss is measured by the difference between the spot rate at the balance sheet date and the spot rate at the date of the contract (or later date when gain or loss was last recognized) times the foreign currency amount.

The discount or premium of the forward contract (original difference between the forward rate and the spot rate at the contract date times the foreign currency amount) shall be accounted for separately from the transaction gains and losses and should be taken into income over the life of the contract.

Gains or losses on speculative forward contracts (contracts which are not hedges) are measured by the difference between the forward rate available in the market and the contracted rate (or rate used after the contract date to record gain or loss) times the foreign currency amount. No discount of premium shall be recorded for speculative forward contracts.

Transaction Gains and Losses to be Excluded from Determination of Net Income

Two types of foreign currency transactions have been identified for which gains and losses should be treated as translation adjustments (i.e., to equity) rather than to be taken to income:

a. Foreign currency transactions that are identified as, and are effective as, hedges of an investment in a foreign entity

b. Long term intercompany investments when the entities are consolidated, combined or accounted for by the equity method.

When a forward contract hedges an identifiable commitment, gain or loss on the contract shall be deferred and used to measure the foreign currency transaction upon settlement. Losses should not be deferred if they would be recognized in a later period. The forward contract will be considered a hedge for purposes of gain or loss deferral if both of the following are met:

    a. the transaction is identified as, and is effective as, a hedge of a specific foreign currency commitment, and

    b. the commitment is firm.

The gain or loss for the portion of a hedge exceeding the commitment and any related tax effect shall not be deferred nor shall the gain or loss related to the period after the settlement of the commitment be deferred. If a hedge is terminated before settlement of the commitment the deferred gain or loss shall remain deferred until settlement when it should be used to measure the foreign currency transaction.

Income Tax Consequences of Rate Changes

When taxable gains or deductible losses are reported in different periods for tax and accounting purposes, interperiod tax allocation is required. Translation adjustments are also considered timing differences for tax allocation purposes but the provisions of ABP Opinion 23 (Sec. I42) apply to such adjustments which are deemed to be unremitted earnings of a subsidiary, in which case deferred taxes should not be provided. As required by APB Opinion 11 (Sec. I28), deferred taxes related to foreign currency items reported in equity accounts should be allocated to such equity accounts.

Exchange Rates

Exchange rates to be used for applying this Statement are:

    a. Transactions: the rate at which the transaction could be settled or, at a later balance sheet date, the rate at which the receivable or payable could be settled

b. Statements: the rate which would be used to convert currency for the payment of dividends.

If an exchange rate can not be established for the date it is required the first rate that can be established subsequent to that date should be used.

Disclosure

The aggregate transaction gain or loss, including those of forward contracts, shall be disclosed. Dealers in foreign exchange may elect to disclose these gains and losses as dealer gains and losses.

Changes in cumulative translation adjustments in equity shall be disclosed including the beginning and ending balances, adjustment for the period, taxes allocated for the period and transfers for determining gain or loss on sale or liquidation of an investee.

Sources for this topic in FASB *Accounting Standards: Current Text*:
    ARB 43, Chap. 12

PROFILE:

- Earnings from foreign operations are best reported only when funds have been received.
- Full disclosure is required of foreign subsidiaries whether consolidated or not.

DISCLOSURE:

- See the text following.

This chapter of ARB 43 deals with the recognition of income earned by foreign operations and the consolidation process of foreign subsidiaries.

Earnings of U.S. companies from their foreign operations are best reported only to the extent that funds have been received in the United States or are unrestricted for transfer to the United States. Earnings reported in excess of amounts received in the United States should be disclosed.

Known losses should be provided for. Significant amounts of assets should be disclosed when realization is in jeopardy.

Consolidation of Foreign Subsidiaries

After careful consideration of whether foreign subsidiaries should be consolidated, the following are alternative ways of presenting information on foreign subsidiaries:

1. Do not consolidate the foreign subsidiary and present a supplementary schedule of the foreign subsidiary's assets, liabilities, income, and losses with an indication of the parent's interest.

2. Consolidate the foreign subsidiary and present the same supplementary information as in item 1.

3. Issue two sets of consolidated statements: one set including the foreign subsidiary and the other set excluding the foreign subsidiary.

4. Consolidate the foreign subsidiary and issue parent company statements, showing the income and investment separately for the foreign subsidiary.

Sources for this topic in FASB *Accounting Standards: Current Text*:

APB Opinion 30

PROFILE:

- Gains and losses from disposal of a segment of a business *and* income or loss from operations of that segment should be reported separately from income from continuing operations.

DISCLOSURE:

- Five detailed items are required in year of disposal. See text following.

Reporting for the disposal of a segment of a business (defined as a unit readily identifiable by its product or market) should be:

Income from continuing operations		$XXX,XXX
Discontinued operations (Note X):		
Loss from operations of discontinued Division Z (less taxes of $XX,XXX)	$XX,XXX	
Loss on disposal of Division Z (less taxes of $XX,XXX)	XX,XXX	XX,XXX
Net income		$XXX,XXX

This discontinued operations section of the income statement should appear before extraordinary items and cumulative effect of accounting changes, if any.

Two significant dates are defined:

1. Measurement date: the date the decision to dispose of the segment is made
2. Disposal date: the date a sale is final or the date operations stop if the segment is abandoned rather than sold

These dates are important because loss on disposal is calculated and recognized as of the measurement date if a loss is indicated. If a gain on disposal is indicated, it should be recognized only when it is realized, which generally is the disposal date.

If operations continue between measurement and disposal dates, estimated losses from operations should be added to the recognized loss on disposal at the measurement date, but estimated income from operations should offset estimated loss from disposal only to the extent of that estimated loss. Estimated income from operations after the measurement date in excess of estimated loss on disposal should be recognized only when realized.

Costs incurred directly and specifically because of the decision to dispose of the segment should be included in the gain or loss on the disposal.

Disclosure.   In addition to the display above, notes to the financial statements for the year of the measurement date shall include:

a) identification of the segment
b) anticipated disposal date
c) method of disposal (sale, abandonment, etc)
d) indication of the assets and liabilities on the balance sheet remaining to be disposed of
e) income or loss and proceeds from disposal subsequent to the measurement date.

Similar information should also be reported in the period of disposal if subsequent to the period including the measurement date.

Sources for this topic in FASB *Accounting Standards: Current Text*:

APB Opinions 9, 11, 30
FASB Statements 4, 44

PROFILE:

- Extraordinary items must be unusual *and* infrequent. Six specific items are excluded from extraordinary classification. See Sec. I22 for presentation of items not meeting both of these criteria.

DISCLOSURE:

- The nature of the item, calculation of the gain or loss, and the related income taxes should be disclosed.

Extraordinary items are defined as those which are *both* unusual and occur infrequently. Gains and losses which specifically should not be reported as extraordinary are:

1. Write-down or write-off of receivables, inventory, equipment leased to others and intangibles.
2. Foreign exchange or translation, including devaluations.
3. Disposal of a segment of a business.
4. Sale or abandonment of assets used in the business.
5. Effects of strikes.
6. Adjustment of long-term contract accruals.

Disclosure.   Extraordinary items should be reported, net of taxes, as the last item on the income statement before net income (unless there is a cumulative effect of accounting change in which case the extraordinary item is reported above the cumulative effect of the change). For example:

Income before extraordinary items	$XXX,XXX
Extraordinary loss (less related income taxes of $XX,XXX) (Note X)	XX,XXX
Net Income	$XXX,XXX

Sources for this topic in FASB *Accounting Standards: Current Text*:
   APB Opinion 30

PROFILE:
- Gains and losses which are unusual or infrequent (not both), and thus do not qualify for extraordinary classification, should be reported as separate items as part of income from continuing operations. These items should NOT be reported net of tax.

DISCLOSURE:
- The nature and financial effect of the item should be disclosed on the income statement or in the notes.

Sources for this topic in FASB *Accounting Standards: Current Text*:
    APB Opinions 10, 11

PROFILE:
- Comprehensive interperiod tax allocation is required.
- Intraperiod tax allocation is required for selected items.
- Deferred taxes must not be discounted to give effect to the time value of money (except where such discounting was used prior to September 26, 1966).

DISCLOSURE:
- See Sec. I28, Income Taxes: Financial Reporting.

Timing Differences

1. Comprehensive interperiod tax allocation is required and must be applied to all timing differences, which are defined as those items that affect taxable income in a different period than that recognized for accounting income.

2. The deferred method of tax allocation must be used. This method uses the tax rate existing when the timing difference arises, is not changed for subsequent tax rate changes, and results in deferred tax credits or charges which are amortized in future periods as the timing differences reverse.

3. The tax effect must be calculated by determining income taxes before and after the item resulting in the timing difference.

4. The tax effects of timing differences may be determined for each item separately or similar items may be combined. If combined, the change in deferred taxes may be determined by either:

   a. Combining new timing differences at current tax rates with reversals at the original rates, or

   b. Applying the current tax rate to the net change in timing differences

Tax Allocation Within a Period

Intraperiod tax allocation should be used so as to report the proper after-tax effect of income before extraordinary items, extraordinary items, prior period adjustments, and items affecting equity accounts.

Sources for this topic in FASB *Accounting Standards: Current Text*:

APB Opinions 10, 11

FASB Statement 37

PROFILE:

- The balance sheet must show net current and net noncurrent deferred taxes as indicated by the "related" asset or liability.
- The income statement must show tax amounts as payable and deferred.
- Loss carryforwards recognized in subsequent periods should be reported as extraordinary items.

DISCLOSURE:

- Additional disclosures are required for loss carryforwards. See the text which follows.

Financial Reporting—General

The balance sheet must show net current deferred taxes and net noncurrent deferred taxes. "Net of tax" reporting of timing differences is not acceptable accounting.

If a reduction in an asset or liability causes a timing difference to reverse, the deferred tax account is "related." Deferred taxes are classified current or noncurrent the same as their related asset or liability.

When a deferred tax account is not related to an asset or liability it must be classified according to the expected reversal date.

Income tax expense for the period must be separated, in the statement or the footnotes, into the amount currently payable and the effects of timing differences and operating losses.

Operating Losses

The tax effect of recognized loss carrybacks and carryforwards must be classified as current or noncurrent, depending on expected realization.

Loss carryforwards not recognized in the loss period, which are realized subsequently, shall be recognized as extraordinary items.

Additional disclosures:

1. Amounts and date of expiration of unrecognized loss carryforwards and an indication of amounts that will be restored to deferred tax credits

2. Amounts and date of expiration of material other unused tax benefits

3. Explanation of differences between income before taxes and taxable income and variations in the relationship between income before taxes and tax expense

Sources for this topic in FASB *Accounting Standards: Current Text*:
APB Opinions 2, 4
FASB Interpretations 25, 32
FASB Technical Bulletin 81–2

PROFILE:

- These Opinions point out the two acceptable methods of treating the investment credit: directly to income and over the life of the asset acquired.

DISCLOSURE:

- When the investment credit is material, disclosure must be made of the method of accounting used and the amounts. Amounts of unused investment credit must also be disclosed.

There are two acceptable methods for accounting for the investment credit:

1. Taken into income over the life of the asset (preferable)
2. Taken into income when realized as a reduction of the income tax provision

When amortized over the life of the asset the investment credit may be classified on the balance sheet as either:

1. A reduction of the related asset (preferable), or
2. Deferred income

Financial statements shall reflect only the amount of credit used to offset the tax liability plus the amount carried back where a claim for refund exists. Unused credit that may be carried forward should affect the accounts only as the credit is realized.

Interpretation 25

This interpretation does not affect entities that recognize the investment credit over the life of the asset.

For entities taking the investment credit into income in the year realized, such investment credit shall be recognized as a reduction of income tax expense. This expense reduction is calculated as if the tax liability was calculated on pretax accounting income after permanent differences. Tax expense shall be reduced further by eliminating other deferred tax credits up to the amount of such other deferred credits which will reverse during the investment credit carryforward period. When the tax benefits of the investment credits of the previous sentence are realized, the other deferred tax credits that were eliminated should be restored.

When unused investment credits are acquired in a purchase business combination, the following rules apply:

1. Goodwill must be reduced in the period when such investment credit is realized and remaining goodwill must be amortized for the current and future periods. (No prior period adjustments are permitted.)
2. If there is no goodwill to absorb the credit for realization of the investment credit, other noncurrent assets (exclusive of investments in securities) must be reduced.

3. When no goodwill or other noncurrent assets are present to absorb the credit a deferred credit must be established and amortized to income over a period of not more than forty years.

Interpretation 32

Recognition of unused investment credit shall be limited by the federal percentage limitations that apply for the year for which such calculation is being made.

Sources for this topic in FASB *Accounting Standards: Current Text*:

APB Opinion 11
FASB Interpretation 25

PROFILE:

- This portion of Opinion 11 specifies how carrybacks and carryforwards are to be treated for accounting purposes. Generally carryovers are recognized only upon realization but criteria are presented for recognition of unrealized carryforwards.

DISCLOSURE:

- See Sec I28, Income Taxes: Financial Reporting.

Operating losses that may be carried back for refunds must be recognized in net income of the period of the loss.

Operating loss carryforwards must not be recognized until they are realized except in those circumstances where realization is certain. When carryforward losses are realized in subsequent periods, recognition must be as an extraordinary item.

In those rare instances when loss carryfowards may be recognized in the year of the loss (the loss is an isolated, unusual event and future income is almost certain), recognition of the tax effects of the loss must be at rates expected to be in effect when the carryforward is realized. If tax rates change from that which was expected, any difference must be taken to income tax expense in the year the carryforward is realized.

When a loss carryforward arises and deferred tax credits exist, accounting treatment depends on whether or not the carryforward is recognized:

1. If the loss carryforward is not recognized (the usual case), deferred tax credits must be written off. This write-off must not exceed the lower of the tax effect of the loss carryforward or the total of deferred tax credit amortization that would have been recorded during the carryforward period. As the loss carryforward is realized in subsequent periods the deferred tax credits so eliminated must be restored.

2. If the loss carryforward is recognized in the period of the loss, amortization of deferred tax credits must follow normal procedures for reversal of the related timing differences.

Sources for this topic in FASB *Accounting Standards: Current Text*:
    APB Opinions 23, 24
    FASB Statement 31
    FASB Interpretations 22, 29

PROFILE:
- APB Opinion 23 specifies accounting for income taxes relating to:

    1. Undistributed earnings of subsidiaries
    2. Investments in corporate joint ventures
    3. "Bad debt reserves" of savings and loan associations

- APB Opinion 24 deals with the tax implications of undistributed earnings if investees accounted for under the equity method.
- FASB 31 deals with tax allocation for U.K. Stock Relief.

DISCLOSURE:
- Specified in related subsection following.

APB Opinion 23

Undistributed Earnings of Subsidiaries

Generally, undistributed earnings of a subsidiary are considered to be timing differences and thus require deferred tax accounting. An exception may be made when one of the criteria of indefinite reversal is met. These criteria are:

1. The subsidiary has invested, and will continue to invest, the earnings so they cannot be distributed to the parent.
2. The earnings will be distributed in a tax-free liquidation.

If the election is made and circumstances subsequently change, taxes must be accrued currently and not as an extraordinary item.

When the investee loses subsidiary status but the remaining investment must be accounted for under the equity method, the investor must determine income taxes following the requirements of APB Opinion 24 (see below). If the parent did not recognize tax expense on the undistributed earnings while the investee was a subsidiary (i.e., it qualified for one of the exceptions above), as soon as subsidiary status is lost the parent must accrue taxes on such earnings when it becomes apparent that they will be distributed.

Disclosure regarding lack of tax provision on undistributed earnings of a subsidiary must include an explanation as to which exception criterion was met and the total amount of such earnings on which no tax provision has been made.

Corporate Joint Ventures

Corporate joint ventures that are of a permanent nature and which are accounted for using the equity method are essentially the same as subsidiaries with respect to undistributed earnings. Accordingly, accounting for timing differences and disclosure should be the same for these ventures as the requirements for subsidiaries listed above.

Bad Debt Reserves of Savings and Loan Associations

Bad debt provisions which are accounted for in general reserves and which differ significantly from the bad debts provision used to arrive at pretax accounting income are permanent differences and do not require deferred tax accounting. Taxes must be accrued, however, if it later appears that the reserve is, or will be, reduced. Such taxes must not be an extraordinary item.

Disclosure for such bad debt reserves accounted for in general reserves must include:

1. Purpose for the reserves
2. Indication that taxes could become payable in the future
3. Total amount of the reserve on which tax provisions have not been made

APB Opinion 24

Differences between accounting income under the equity method and taxable income due to undistributed earnings of an investee are timing differences and require deferred tax accounting. Note that the conclusion here does not apply to subsidiaries or joint ventures and that the indefinite reversal criteria is not applicable where control does not exist (see APB Opinion 23 above).

The investor must accrue taxes as appropriate to the form in which such undistributed earnings will be realized. If it is expected that dividends will be received, ordinary tax rates must be used. If the earnings are expected to be realized by disposition of the investment, capital gains rates must be used. In either case applicable deductions and credits must be taken into consideration.

If the difference in accounting income and taxable income results from losses of the investee, the rules of accounting for operating losses in APB Opinion 11 (Sec. I37) apply.

When ownership of an investee increases to subsidiary status, previously accrued deferred taxes shall be taken into income only as dividends received exceed the share of earnings subsequent to achieving subsidiary status. Similarly, when ownership falls to the point where the cost method is required, previously accrued deferred taxes shall be included in income only as dividends are received in excess of the investor's share of investee's earnings subsequent to the date of the change.

FASB Statement 31

This Statement deals with the question of whether the special tax relief granted by the United Kingdom for increases in inventory values should be a timing difference or a permanent difference.

The tax benefits of this "stock relief" must be deferred unless it is expected that the benefit will not be recaptured before the six-year recapture period expires. When circumstances change and it later appears that the benefit will not be recaptured after it was deferred, the benefit must be used to reduce tax expense in the period such determination is made. If the benefit was not deferred and it later becomes appropriate to defer it, such adjustment must increase tax expense in the period such determination is made.

For interim purposes the effects of a change in status of the stock relief benefit should be considered in determining the effective annual tax rate when accruing income taxes.

Disclosure of the circumstances must be made when application of this Statement creates a material distortion of the usual relationship between tax expense and pretax income.

Interpretation 22

Income tax benefits related to railroad grading and tunnel bores are timing differences and thus require comprehensive tax allocation. The indefinite reversal criteria is thus not applicable to these items.

Interpretation 29

When operating loss carryforwards related to an investee have not been recognized, a question arises as to whether the tax benefits realized on disposition of the investee should be extraordinary credits or reductions in the income tax provision. The tax benefits must be classified with the gain or loss on sale of the investment.

Sources for this topic in FASB *Accounting Standards: Current Text*:
> ARB 43, Chap. 5
> APB Opinions 6, 17
> FASB Statement 44
> FASB Interpretation 9

PROFILE:

- Intangibles must be recorded at cost.
- All intangibles must be amortized over not more than forty years.
- Motor carriers subject to the Motor Carrier Act of 1980 must write off intangible operating rights made worthless by deregulation of the industry.

DISCLOSURE:

- No special requirements

APB Opinion 17

Intangible assets acquired or developed must be recorded at cost. Excluded from intangible assets are costs incurred to develop and maintain intangibles which are not specifically identifiable or have indefinite lives. Costs for these latter intangibles must be expensed when incurred.

When intangible assets are acquired with other assets a distinction should be made between identifiable and unidentifiable intangibles. The identifiable intangibles must be allocated a portion of the total purchase cost based on fair values. The unidentifiable intangibles (generally goodwill) are valued as the excess of the total cost of the group of assets over the fair values of all of the tangible and identifiable intangible assets.

The cost of intangible assets must be systematically amortized to income, preferably on a straight-line basis, over the useful life of the asset or forty years, whichever is shorter. Intangibles must not be written off arbitrarily in the year costs are incurred.

When a material portion of assets are disposed of, any related goodwill that was recognized in the acquisition of such assets must also be removed from the accounts.

FASB Statement 44

Motor carriers subject to the Motor Carrier Act of 1980 must separate their intangibles into three categories:

1. Interstate operating rights
2. Other identifiable intangibles
3. Goodwill

The basis for classification is the conditions that existed when the intangibles were acquired. If separation is not possible, the total cost shall be deemed interstate operating rights.

Unamortized interstate operating rights (which are worthless under the Act) shall be charged to income (extraordinary if material) and may not be retroactively applied by restatement of prior financial statements.

Other identifiable intangibles and goodwill shall continue to be accounted for under APB Opinion 17.

Sources for this topic in FASB *Accounting Standards: Current Text*:

FASB Statements 34, 42, 58

FASB Interpretation 33

FASB Technical Bulletin 81–5

PROFILE:

- This Standard presents the rules for the capitalization of interest related to the acquisition of assets. Details are given about the types of qualifying assets, amount of interest that may be capitalized, and the period for which capitalization is applicable.

DISCLOSURE:

- Disclosure is required of interest cost incurred, expensed, and capitalized.

Interest is a normal cost of acquiring assets and bringing them to the condition and location where they will be used. Interest must be capitalized when incurred in the acquisition of qualifying assets unless the amount is immaterial.

Qualifying Assets

Interest must be capitalized for:

1. Assets constructed for internal use
2. Assets constructed for sale or lease if for identifiable projects
3. Investments accounted for by the equity method while organizing to begin planned operations.

Interest must not be capitalized for:

1. Normal inventories produced in large, repetitive production runs
2. Assets in use or ready for use in internal operations
3. Assets not being used, or being made ready for use, for revenue generation activities
4. Assets not included in the consolidated balance sheet
5. Investments accounted for by the equity method after the investee has begun operations
6. Investments in regulated companies which capitalize the cost of debt and equity.

Amount of Interest

Capitalizeable interest is the marginal interest incurred during the asset acquisition period (i.e., incremental interest incurred that would not have been incurred if the asset had not been acquired).

The amount of interest capitalized shall be calculated by applying the entity's external borrowing rate for the period to the average cumulative expenditures for the asset. The external borrowing rate should be the rate of specific financing for the asset acquisition or a weighted average of this financing plus other financing if the specific financing is less than the average cumulative expenditures. In no circumstances shall the interest capitalized exceed the total interest incurred by the entity for the period.

Capitalization Period

The period for interest capitalization shall begin and continue as long as the following three conditions are present:

1. Expenditures have been made.
2. The asset is being prepared for use.
3. Interest is being incurred.

This period concludes with the completion of the asset for its intended use.

Disclosures

The following shall be disclosed in the financial statements or notes:

1. Interest cost incurred
2. Interest charged to expense (if none is capitalized), or
3. Interest capitalized (if any)

Interpretation 33

For oil- and gas-producing companies, interest may be capitalized only on:

1. Extraordinarily large investments in unproved properties
2. Major development projects

In both cases the asset costs should not be currently amortized and development or exploration must be in progress.

Sources for this topic in FASB *Accounting Standards: Current Text*:

APB Opinions 12, 21

FASB Statement 34

PROFILE:

- Receivables and payables must be carried at the discounted present value of future payments.
- The "interest" method of amortizing premium or discount on long-term debt is acceptable accounting.

DISCLOSURE:

- The method of display is indicated but no other special requirements are specified.

When a note is exchanged for cash, its present value is deemed to be equal to such proceeds.

Generally, the exchange of a note for property or services in an arm's-length transaction, which contains an interest provision, should be assumed to represent a fair return to the provider of funds. When, however, the interest rate is not stated or is unreasonable or when the face value of the note is materially different from the cash equivalent of the items exchanged, it will be necessary to record the transaction at the fair value of the note or items exchanged, whichever is more clearly evident. In these circumstances, any premium or discount from the face of the note must be accounted for as interest over the period of the note. When fair values of neither the note nor the items exchanged can be determined, the note must be valued by discounting all payments to present value using an imputed interest rate determined at the time of the exchange.

The interest rate for discounting the future payments should be selected as close as possible to the rate that would be paid for borrowing in similar transactions with similar risks. The Opinion does not specify particular rates but describes the considerations that may affect the selection.

When interest has been imputed, the difference between the face of the note and its present value must be recorded as premium or discount and amortized as interest to establish a constant rate of interest on the declining book value of the note.

Disclosure: The note must be reported with its associated premium or discount. The face amount and the effective interest rate must be disclosed. Amortization of premium or discount must be combined with interest in the income statement and issue costs must be carried on the balance sheet as deferred charges.

Sources for this topic in FASB *Accounting Standards: Current Text*:
   APB Opinion 28
   FASB Statements 3, 16
   FASB Interpretation 18
   FASB Technical Bulletin 79-9

PROFILE:

-   Accounting principles for interim periods must be the same as used for annual financial statements. The opinion provides for exceptions for results that otherwise might be misleading (e.g., inventory market declines, LIFO liquidations, standard cost variances, etc.).
-   Income taxes must be provided using an estimated effective annual tax rate.
-   Accounting changes requiring cumulative effect adjustments must be reported in the first interim period even if this requires restatement of prior interim periods when the change is made in other than the first period.

DISCLOSURE:

-   Several disclosures are required if interim financial statements would be misleading without them.
-   Comprehensive disclosure is required in the interim period of the change and certain information is required after the change.

APB Opinion 28

Standards for Interim Reports

Interim periods are considered integral parts of the annual accounting period, which means that, generally, the same accounting principles used for annual financial statements must be used for interim financial statements. This is particularly true for revenues and the costs and expenses that are directly related to the generation of that revenue.

Several exceptions to this rule relate to inventories:

1. The gross profit method of estimating inventory is acceptable for interim financial statements with disclosure of the method used.

2. When LIFO layers have been liquidated in interim periods but are expected to be replaced by year-end, inventory and cost of sales for the interim period must be increased by the estimated cost of replacing the liquidated inventory.

3. Temporary market declines of inventory prices must not be recognized at interim if prices are reasonably expected to recover by year-end. When market declines have been recognized and the market recovers in a later interim period, such recovery must be recorded as a gain to the extent of previously recognized losses.

4. Variances from standard costs should be treated in interim periods in the same way that they are treated at year-end except that variances that are expected to be absorbed by year-end should be deferred for interim reporting.

Accounting for costs and expenses other than product costs presents some difficulties for interim reporting which are not present for annual periods. These costs and expenses should be treated as follows:

1. The costs must either be charged to the interim period when incurred or be allocated to those interim periods that benefit from the cost (but such an allocation should not be arbitrary).

2. If the cost cannot be matched with benefits of other interim periods, it must be expensed as incurred. These costs should be disclosed unless similar costs are included in the prior year interim period presented for comparison.

3. Gains and losses of the type that would be recognized at year-end must be recognized in the interim period in which they occur.

4. Certain costs and expenses typically require year-end adjustments (e.g., inventory shrinkage, bad debts, quantity discounts, and bonuses) even though they could be estimated at interim periods. Such costs must be estimated, if possible, and assigned to interim periods.

Seasonal variations in revenues, costs, and expenses should be disclosed to dispel unwarranted inferences that readers may draw about how indicative interim results are for annual results.

Income taxes should be provided for in interim periods by estimating the annual effective tax rate (considering all allowable credits, deductions, exclusions, etc.) and applying this rate to year-to-date income. Care should be taken in developing this rate to allow for normal intraperiod allocation of income taxes to items to be reported net of tax.

The tax benefits of operating losses that cannot be carried back should be recognized only when realization of the benefits is assured. When such tax benefits were not recognized in an earlier interim period and subsequent operations are profitable, no tax expense should be recorded in the later interim period until the unrecognized losses are fully offset. (See also FASB Interp. 18, which follows.)

Disposals of a segment of a business, extraordinary items, and unusual or infrequently occurring events must be reported separately in the period in which they occur and not prorated over the remaining fiscal year. Contingencies must also be reported in the same manner as they would be at year-end.

Accounting changes, in general, must be treated in accordance with APB Opinion 20 (Sec. A06). Certain changes in accounting principle, changes in entity, prior period adjustments, and correction of errors all require restatement of previously issued financial statements, which is now expanded to include previously issued interim financial statements. Changes in estimates must be made prospectively (i.e., current and future interim and annual periods). Changes in accounting principle requiring a cumulative effect adjustment are covered in FASB Statement 3 (which follows).

Disclosure by Publicly Traded Companies

When publicly traded companies provide summarized financial information rather than financial statements at interim periods, the following minimum information must be issued regarding the current quarter and year to date together with comparable data for the prior year:

1. Revenues, tax expense, extraordinary items and their tax effect, cumulative effect of changes in accounting principles, and net income
2. Primary and fully diluted earnings per share
3. Information of the seasonality of revenue, cost, and expenses
4. Material changes in income taxes
5. Segment disposal, extraordinary items, and unusual or infrequent items
6. Contingencies
7. Accounting changes
8. Major changes in financial position

When major events have occurred in the fourth quarter and a separate fourth-quarter report is not issued, information about those major events must be disclosed in a note to the annual financial statements.

Interpretation 18

An entity must develop an effective annual tax rate which takes into account the investment credit, foreign tax rates, capital gains rates, percentage depletion, and any other items affecting the annual tax liability. This rate should be applied to the ordinary income (i.e., income exclusive of items requiring intraperiod tax allocation) for the year to date and the current interim provision (or benefit) adjusted as necessary.

If a positive income is expected for the year but the entity has a loss for the year to date, the tax benefit for such loss may only be recognized if its realization is assured beyond a reasonable doubt. When realization of the tax benefit is not assured, deferred tax credits due to timing differences must be adjusted as required by APB Opinion 11 (Sec. I37).

When an ordinary loss is expected for the year, interim tax or benefit must be calculated using the effective annual tax rate described above. The tax benefit for the year, however, should not exceed the amount that is realizable. When the annual benefit is not assured, existing deferred tax credits due to timing differences must be adjusted as required by APB Opinion 11 (Sec. I37).

Tax provisions (benefits) and financial statement display for unusual, infrequent, and extraordinary items and discontinued operations shall be the same for interim periods as required by APB Opinion 11 for annual periods. The tax or benefit is determined by calculating the tax liability with and without the item in question. An exception relates to the recognition of tax benefits of loss items when realization is not assured. In this case deferred tax credits due to timing differences must be adjusted as required by APB Opinion 11 (Sec. I37).

Tax benefits of operating loss carryforwards shall be recognized as extraordinary items in interim periods where positive income is recorded.

When an entity is subject to taxes in several jurisdictions on income identified by jurisdiction, the interim tax provision shall be made using a single estimated annual tax rate unless:

1. A loss is anticipated in a jurisdiction for which no benefits may be recognized. In this case interim tax provisions should be determined by separately applying the rules to the operations in that jurisdiction and the operations for the balance of the entity.

2. An entity is unable to estimate the income or the tax for a foreign jurisdiction. In these circumstances the tax should be recognized in the interim period when income is reported from operations in that jurisdiction and the overall effective tax rate should be developed ignoring these operations.

When new legislation affects tax provisions for the current year, the annual effective tax rate must be revised and the new rate used for the next year-to-date tax calculation.

When there is a significant variation in the normal relationship between tax expense and accounting income, the reasons for such variation must be disclosed.

FASB Statement 3

Changes in Accounting Principle (Other than to LIFO)

Cumulative-effect-type accounting changes in interim reports must be reported in the first interim period for the year. If the change is not made until a subsequent quarter, application of the rule requires a restatement of all interim periods of the year to date to reflect:

1. The cumulative effect in income for the first quarter
2. Use of the new principle for each quarter of the current year

Disclosure of such accounting changes requires the following information in the interim financial reports:

1. In the period in which the change is made:
    a. The nature and justification of the change
    b. The effect of the change on income from continuing operations, net income, and earnings per share
    c. Pro forma figures for income from continuing operations, net income, and earnings per share for the current period and any interim periods of prior years which are presented
    d. If the change is made after the first interim period, the effect of the change on, and the absolute amount of, income from continuing operations, net income, and earnings per share for each interim period prior to the change
2. In periods subsequent to the change, disclosure must indicate the effect of the change on income from continuing operations, net income, and earnings per share.

Changes to LIFO

The principles described above apply to changes to the LIFO method of inventory valuation (except for pro forma figures which would be impossible to determine) when such change is made in the first interim period. When the change to LIFO is made past the first quarter, the disclosures discussed above are required *and* prior interim periods must be restated using the new principle.

FASB Statement 16

Adjustments related to current and prior interim periods should be reported by distributing the adjustment, as appropriate, to:

1. The current interim period
2. Prior interim periods resulting in a restatement of income for those prior interim periods
3. The first interim period for the portion of the adjustment relating to prior fiscal years

Disclosure of the effects of these changes shall be made, in the period the adjustment is made, on income from continuing operations, net income, and the related per share amounts for each interim period affected.

Sources for this topic in FASB *Accounting Standards: Current Text*:
ARB 43, Chap. 4

PROFILE:
- This chapter presents ten basic principles regarding accounting for inventory.

DISCLOSURE:
- Disclosure of the inventory method is required with additional disclosures when the method is changed (governed by APB Opinion 20, Sec. A06).

1. Inventory includes materials, supplies, work in process, and product or merchandise available for sale.
2. Inventory accounting should yield a proper income figure through the matching of revenue and expense.
3. Inventory must be accounted for at cost.
4. Inventory cost may be determined by any of several cost flow assumptions (e.g., FIFO, LIFO, average) and the method selected should clearly reflect income.
5. Inventory must be written down to market when cost does not reflect utility value of the inventory.
6. Market value, for inventory purposes, must not be greater than normal selling price reduced by costs to complete and sell the item nor less than this ceiling reduced by a normal profit margin.
7. "Cost or market, whichever is lower" may be applied to individual items, categories of items, or the total inventory.
8. Inventory methods must be consistently applied and such method disclosed. Significant changes in inventory method must be disclosed as described in APB Opinion 20, Accounting Changes (Sec. A06).
9. Inventory may be stated above cost only when there is a fixed market at fixed prices and no significant disposal costs to be incurred. Full disclosure is required when inventory is stated above cost.
10. Losses on purchase commitments must be recorded and disclosed.

Sources for this topic in FASB *Accounting Standards: Current Text*:
    APB Opinion 18
    FASB Interpretation 35
    FASB Technical Bulletin 79–19

PROFILE:
- The equity method is required for all unconsolidated subsidiaries, corporate joint ventures, and major investments (over 20% owned).
- Application of the equity method results in income substantially equal to consolidation of the share of ownership in an investee.

DISCLOSURE:
- Specific information about each investee is required; see the text.

Uses of the Equity Method

The equity method should be used for:

1. All subsidiaries that are not consolidated
2. Corporate joint ventures
3. Investees where the investor can influence the policies of the investee (i.e., generally where the investor owns 20% or more of the investee's stock)

Application of the Equity Method

The equity method must be applied to yield the same results as would obtain if the investee were a consolidated subsidiary:

1. Intercompany profits and losses must be eliminated.
2. The difference between cost and equity in net assets must be amortized.
3. Capital transactions of the investee affecting the investor's equity must be treated as if the investee were a consolidated subsidiary.

The investment balance and the share of earnings (or losses) shall each be reported as single amounts in the respective investor financial statements. If the investee reports extraordinary items and/or prior period adjustments, the investor's share shall be reported separately if material to the investor.

Gains and losses from sale of shares of an investee are measured by the difference between the proceeds and the carrying value of the shares.

Permanent loss in value of the investee must be recognized. If recognition of operating losses of the investee reduces the investment to zero, the equity method must be discontinued unless the investor has guaranteed obligations of the investee. Subsequent profits of the investee should be recognized only after unrecognized losses have been recovered by the investee.

Equity in earnings of the investee should be recognized only after a provision for cumulative preferred dividends of the investee.

When the ownership share of an investee falls below the minimum for application of the equity method (20%), use of the equity method must be discontinued without retroactive adjustment of the carrying amount of the investment. When subsequent dividends are received in excess of the new lower ownership share of earnings, the excess dividends must be used to reduce the investment rather than recorded as dividend income.

When the ownership share of an investee rises to the point where the equity method is required, retroactive adjustment of the investment and retained earnings accounts must be made to reflect the equity method since acquisition.

Disclosure

The following disclosures are required for investments accounted for under the equity method:

1. Names and percentage owned of each investee
2. Investor's accounting policies for the investments
3. Any difference between book value and share of investees' assets and how such difference is accounted for
4. Market value of the investment, if available

When unconsolidated subsidiaries, corporate joint ventures, and other less-than-50%-owned investees are material to the financial position or results of operations of the investor, summarized information of financial position and operations of these investees must be disclosed.

When an investor's share of an investee can be significantly diluted through conversion or exercise of investee's convertible securities, options, warrants, and so on, pro forma effects of these possible actions on the investor must be disclosed.

Interpretation 35

This interpretation reiterates the position of APB Opinion 18 that the equity method of accounting for an investee is required when the investor can exercise significant influence over the investee. The presumption that an investor with a 20% interest can exercise significant influence is still valid until substantial evidence in a particular case indicates otherwise.

Examples of evidence that *may* indicate an inability to exercise significant influence over an investee are:

1. Overt opposition by the investee through the courts or regulatory agencies

2. Contractual surrender of significant rights of the investor to the investee

3. Concentration of a majority of ownership in the investee which ignores the views of the investor

4. Inability of the investor to secure necessary financial information from the investee to apply the equity method

5. Trial and failure to obtain representation on the investee's board of directors

Although this list is not exhaustive, none of the examples above is conclusive evidence that the investor cannot exercise significant influence over the investee. All of the facts in the circumstances must be evaluated before a judgment is reached.

Sources for this topic in FASB *Accounting Standards: Current Text*:
  ARB 43
  FASB Statement 12
  FASB Interpretation 10, 11, 12, 13, 16
  FASB Technical Bulletin 79–19

PROFILE:

- Separate current and noncurrent portfolios are required for marketable equity securities.
- Each portfolio is to be valued at the lower of aggregate cost or market, using a valuation allowance account if market is lower.
- Changes in the valuation allowance for the current portfolio are to be reported in net income, while the balance of the valuation allowance for the noncurrent portfolio is to be reported in the stockholders' equity section.

DISCLOSURE:

- Several detailed disclosures are required regarding cost, market values, and realized and unrealized gains and losses.

Enterprises Not Subject to Special Industry Practices

Marketable equity securities must be separated into both current and noncurrent portfolios and each portfolio reported at the lower of aggregate cost or market at the balance sheet date. If the balance sheet is unclassified, the marketable equity securities are to be treated as all noncurrent for applying the following rules. When the aggregate market value of a portfolio is less than cost, the difference below cost must be recorded in a valuation allowance account.

Increases in the valuation allowance for the current portfolio must be charged to income for the period as unrealized losses. Subsequent decreases in the valuation allowance must be included in income for the period as recoveries of unrealized losses, but such recoveries are limited to the amounts previously charged to income.

The valuation allowance for the noncurrent portfolio is established by creation of an unrealized loss account which must be reported in the equity section of the balance sheet. Recoveries of market values must be accounted for as reductions in the valuation allowance and a corresponding reduction in the unrealized loss of the equity section.

Realized gains and losses must affect income when they occur regardless of the current–noncurrent status of securities portfolios.

When the noncurrent portfolio is valued at less than cost and the market decline is not temporary, the loss must be accounted for as a realized loss, resulting in a new, lower-cost basis for these securities.

Transfers between portfolios must be recorded at the lower of cost or market and losses must be recorded as realized losses when market is lower than cost.

Disclosure

1. For each balance sheet presented: the aggregate cost and market value for each portfolio and an indication as to the carrying amount of the portfolio
2. For each income statement presented: the net unrealized gain or

loss in income and the basis used (average, etc.) to determine cost for measuring such gain or loss

3. At the balance sheet date of the current period: the gross unrealized gains for securities where market exceeds cost and the gross unrealized loss for securities where cost exceeds market

Special Industry Practices

Generally, this Statement does not require departure from accepted industry practices except for the following:

1. When the practice has been to value securities at cost, marketable equity securities are now required to be valued at the lower of aggregate cost or market.

2. When the industry practice adopted does not recognize unrealized losses in income but does include them in the equity section, certain additional disclosures are required:

   a. Gross unrealized gains and losses at the current balance sheet date

   b. Change in the net unrealized gain or loss for each period presented

The Statement does not require an investor and investee (under the equity method or consolidated) to bring their accounting for marketable equity securities into agreement as long as both use acceptable methods. The one exception to this rule requires the investee to include realized gains and losses in income if the investor uses this method.

When a parent company uses special industry practices and two or more subsidiaries do not, the portfolios of the subsidiaries shall be consolidated as separate current and noncurrent portfolios without consideration of the parent's securities in order to determine the lower of aggregate cost or market. Disclosures regarding these securities are the same as required for separate subsidiary financial statements.

Income Taxes

Unrealized gains and losses in both portfolios are defined as timing differences with respect to interperiod income tax allocation and the principles of APB Opinion 11 (Sec. I24, I28) must be applied to determine if such gains or losses should be reduced for the tax effect.

Interpretation 10

Accounting principles provided in FASB Statement 12 are applicable to personal financial statements.

Interpretation 11

The only write-downs of marketable securities for market declines occurring after the balance sheet date are those which may be of a permanent nature for noncurrent portfolios. The subsequent market declines may be further evidence of the nontemporary nature of market declines, which may require taking realized losses on this portfolio.

Interpretation 12

An entity that used an allowance account for market declines before FASB 12 was issued, and which established that allowance by charges to income, must still use the original cost of the securities to measure gains and losses. The original allowance account must be eliminated by a credit to income when this Interpretation is first applied.

If securities were written down because values were impaired prior to implementation of FASB Statement 12, such lower value is "cost" for purposes of applying the Statement.

Interpretation 13

For purposes of measuring aggregate cost and market values of consolidated entities, such aggregates are determined as of the balance sheet date of each company consolidated, even if the dates of all companies are not the same.

Gains and losses, whether realized or unrealized, which occur subsequent to a subsidiary's balance sheet date but prior to the parent's balance sheet date must be disclosed if they are material to the consolidated results of operations or financial position.

Interpretation 16

Equity securities are not marketable if prices are not available or if trading in the stock is restricted. Availability of price is not absent, however, if there is merely a temporary lack of a quotation and if prices are available within a few days of the balance sheet date. If the restriction on trading will be removed within a year, assuming that market prices are available, the security may be considered marketable.

If a change in a security's current–noncurrent status occurs simultaneously with a change in its marketability status, the change shall be treated as a change in current–noncurrent status (i.e., the security is transferred between portfolios at the lower of cost or market, unrealized losses are recorded as realized, and "cost" is set at the market transfer price).

Sources for this topic in FASB *Accounting Standards: Current Text*:

FASB Statements 13, 17, 22, 23, 26, 27, 28, 29

FASB Interpretations 19, 21, 23, 24, 26, 27

FASB Technical Bulletins 79-10, 11, 12, 13, 14, 15, 16

PROFILE:

- These FASB Statements provide accounting and disclosure requirements for leases for both lessees and lessors. Detailed criteria are provided for classification of leases as either capital-type or operating leases and accounting procedures are proscribed for each classification.

DISCLOSURE:

- Disclosure requirements are specified in detail but differ for lessee and lessor; see the text following.

Types of Leases and Classification Criteria

Leases may be broadly categorized as capital-type leases and operating leases. Leases are classified as operating leases unless at least one of the following criteria are met:

1. The lease transfers title to the leased asset.
2. The lease includes a bargain purchase option.
3. The lease covers at least 75% of the useful life of the asset.
4. The present value of the minimum lease payments (excluding executory costs) is equal to or greater than 90% of the excess of the fair value of the property to the lessor over his or her realizable investment credit. Lessors shall discount lease payments using the rate implicit in the lease, while lessees shall generally use their incremental borrowing rate. Lessees shall use the lessor's implicit rate if it is determinable *and* less than the incremental borrowing rate.

Criteria 3 and 4 shall not be used for classifying leases if the lease term begins during the last 25% of an asset's total useful life.

Lessees: A lessee shall classify a lease as a capital lease if it meets at least one of the criteria noted above; otherwise, the lease shall be treated as an operating lease.

Lessors: Capital-type leases for lessors are further classified into sales-type leases, direct financing leases, and leveraged leases. Classification in any of these categories requires that the lease meet at least one of the foregoing four criteria and *both* of the following:

1. Collection of the minimum lease payments is reasonably assured.
2. No major uncertainties exist relative to costs to be incurred by the lessor.

The subclassifications of capital-type leases are defined as follows:

1. Sales-type lease: leases involving manufacturer or dealer profits or losses. A renewal or extension of any lease may only be classified as a sales-type lease (assuming that it qualifies otherwise) if the new transaction occurs near the end of the original lease term.
2. Direct financing lease: leases that do not qualify as sales-type leases

or leveraged leases. The cost (book value, if different) and fair value of the leased asset are equal at inception of the lease.

3. Leveraged lease: leases involving a third party which provides long-term financing. These leases are discussed in detail below under "Special Areas."

When both parties to a lease agree to change a lease such that application of the criteria above would result in a different classification, a new lease is deemed to exist and the criteria above should be applied to such a new lease.

Accounting and Reporting by Lessees

Capital Leases.   Lessees must record a capital lease as both an asset and a liability at the lower of (1) the present value of the minimum lease payments (exclusive of executory costs) or (2) the fair value of the leased asset.

The recorded asset must be depreciated following normal policies for owned assets except that leases which do not transfer title by the end of the lease or do not have a bargain purchase option shall be depreciated over the term of the lease.

Lease payments should systematically reduce the lease liability and set up interest expense consistent with a constant interest rate on the declining obligation. By the end of the lease the liability should be reduced to an amount equal to any guarantee of residual value or penalty for failure to renew the lease.

Subsequent changes to recorded leases include changes in the provisions of a lease, renewal, extension, and cancellation. These changes should be accounted for as follows:

1. Change in provisions: If changes to the lease do not result in a "new" agreement (see above), or if such new agreement is classified a capital lease, the asset and liability shall be changed to bring the liability to the present value of the revised future lease payments calculated using the interest rate of the initial lease. If the changes to a lease result in a "new" agreement and such lease must be classified as an operating lease, the asset and liability shall be removed from the accounts with gain or loss recorded for any difference.

2. Renewal or extension: If a renewal or extension is still considered a capital lease, it shall be accounted for as a change in provisions (above). If a renewal or extension is deemed an operating lease, the original lease shall be accounted for as a capital lease until the end of its term and then the renewal or extension shall be accounted for as an operating lease for the remainder of its term.

3. Termination: When a capital lease is terminated, the asset and liability shall be removed from the accounts with gain or loss recorded for any difference.

Operating Leases.   Operating leases shall result in charges to rent expense as amounts become payable over the lease term.

Disclosures.   Lessees are required to make disclosures regarding leases as follows:

1. For capital leases:
   a. Total assets capitalized under leases
   b. Total future minimum lease payments and amounts to be paid for each of the ensuing five years with deductions for executory costs
   c. Total expected rentals from noncancellable subleases
   d. Contingent rentals incurred included in each income statement presented

2. For operating leases:
   a. Rental expense in each income statement presented with a breakdown of minimum, contingent, and sublease components
   b. Total future minimum rental payments and the amounts to be paid for each of the ensuing five years
   c. Total expected rentals under noncancellable subleases

3. For all leases: a general description of leasing arrangements and details concerning contingent payments, options in the leases, and restrictions on the lessee included in the lease agreements

Accounting and Reporting by Lessors

Sales-type Leases.   Gross investment in the lease shall be recorded at the sum of the minimum lease payments (excluding executory costs)

and the unguaranteed residual value of the leased asset. The net investment in the lease is the present value of the gross investment calculated with the implicit interest rate in the lease. Unearned income is the difference between the gross investment and the net investment and must be amortized over the lease term by the effective interest method.

Revenue from "sale" of the leased property must be recorded at the present value of the minimum lease payments and the cost of sales must be recorded at the cost of the property plus initial direct costs less the present value of the unguaranteed residual value of the leased asset.

Direct Financing Leases.   Gross investment in direct financing leases is the same as for sales-type leases. Unearned income is measured as the difference between the gross investment and the cost of the asset. Initial direct costs must be charged to income as incurred and a similar amount must be transferred from unearned to earned income. The balance of unearned income must be amortized to income over the lease term using the effective interest method.

Specifications Common to Sales-type and Direct Financing Leases

1. Where minimum lease payments include residual guarantees and/or penalties for failure to renew, and a renewal or extension of the lease makes these provisions inoperative, the balances of the receivable and residual value accounts must be revised to the terms of the revised agreement and the net effect taken to the unearned income account.

2. The estimated residual value must be reviewed regularly with losses recorded for permanent impairment and adjustments made to the amortization rate.

3. Changes in leases must be treated as follows:
   a. Changes in provisions: If changes to the lease do not result in a "new" agreement (see above), or if such new agreement is classified as a direct financing lease, the receivable and residual value accounts must be revised with the net effect taken to unearned income. If the changes result in a new agreement which is classified as an operating lease, the

related lease accounts must be eliminated, the asset set up at the lower of original cost, present fair value, or present carrying amount, and any difference taken to income.

b. Renewal or extension (except those in item 1 above):

(1) Where the change is classified as a direct financing lease, the transaction shall be accounted for under the change in provision rules above.

(2) Where the change is classified as an operating lease, the original accounting as a sale-type lease shall be continued to the end of the original term and then the change shall be treated as an operating lease.

(3) Where the change is classified as a sales-type lease and the change occurs near the end of the original term, the change shall be accounted for as a sales-type lease.

c. Termination: Termination of a lease shall be accounted for in the same manner as a change to an operating lease (item 3a above).

Operating Leases.   Accounting for operating leases shall comply with the following rules:

1. The leased asset shall be accounted for and reported in the same manner as other fixed assets.
2. Rental income shall be recorded on an accrual basis.
3. Initial direct costs, if material, shall be deferred and allocated to income over the lease in proportion to rental income.

Third-Party Participation.   The original accounting treatment for a lease should not be changed because of a subsequent sale or assignment of either the lease or the leased asset under sales-type or direct financing leases. Instead, any profit or loss must be recognized for this separate transaction except for (1) transactions between related parties (see below) and (2) transactions with recourse (profit or loss must systematically be recognized over the lease).

The sale of leased assets under operating leases where the seller/lessor retains substantial risks of ownership must be treated as borrowings rather than sales. In this case the liability created must be reduced by appropriate distribution of lessee payments to interest expense and principal reduction using the interest method.

Disclosures. Lessors are required to make the following disclosures if leasing activity is material:

1. For sales-type and direct financing leases:
    a. Composition of net investment in leases (minimum lease payments, unguaranteed residual values, and unearned income)
    b. Amounts of the minimum lease payments due for each of the next five years
    c. Amount of unearned income recognized in the period to offset initial direct costs (direct financing leases only)
    d. Contingent rentals recognized in the period
2. For operating leases:
    a. Cost and accumulated depreciation of leased assets by functional category
    b. Minimum rental income on noncancellable leases in total and for each of the next five years
    c. Contingent rentals recognized in the period
3. A general description of leasing activity

Special Areas: Real Estate

The basic lease classification criteria must be modified when a lease involves real estate. The modification depends on certain characteristics of the property subject to the lease.

Land. When a lease only covers land, only the first two of the four criteria presented (transfer of title or bargain purchase option) are relevant for classification as capital-type leases.

Land and Building. When a lease covers land and building, the accounting treatment varies with the capital lease criteria which are met.

1. If the lease meets either of the first two of the four criteria for capital leases (transfer of title or bargain purchase option), the

lessee must allocate the present value of minimum lease payments to land and building in proportion to the fair values of the
assets, whereas the lessor must account for these assets as a
single unit.

2. If the lease does not meet either of the first two criteria but does
   meet either the third or fourth criteria (75% of economic life or
   90% of fair value), accounting depends on the relative value of
   land to the total assets leased.
   a. Land is less than 25% of total fair value: Both lessee and lessor
      must treat the assets as a single unit.
   b. Land is more than 25% of total fair value: Both lessee and
      lessor must treat the assets separately and both must treat
      the land as an operating lease and the building as a capital-
      type lease (lessors still must apply the additional criteria
      regarding collectibility of the minimum lease payments and
      uncertainties).

Equipment.   When equipment is leased in addition to real estate, an
appropriate portion of lease payments must be attributed to such
equipment and a separate determination made for classification of the
equipment lease.

Part of a Building.   If the cost and fair value of the leased property
can be determined objectively, leases must be treated using the criteria above for "land and building." If fair value cannot be determined,
lessees must only use the 75% of economic life test to classify the
lease. If neither cost nor fair value can be determined, lessors must
account for the lease as an operating lease.

Special Areas: Related Parties

Generally, the relationship between parties to a lease should not
affect accounting for the lease. Where unrealistic terms have been set
it may be necessary to look to the substance of the transaction rather
than its form to achieve fair classification.

Subsidiaries that exist to lease assets to the parent or affiliates
must be consolidated. Profits and losses between either constituents
to a consolidation or investees under the equity method must be
eliminated in the normal manner.

Special Areas: Sale and Leaseback

Profit or loss to the seller/lessee from a sale and leaseback transaction generally must be deferred and recognized over the life of the lease. Recognition of this deferred profit or loss must be an adjustment to the leased asset amortization (capital lease) or rent expense (operating leases).

When the seller/lessee leases back only a portion of the property, the following conditions apply:

1. If only a minor portion of the property is leased back (10% or less), separate transactions for the sale and lease shall be recorded with the total profit or loss recognized on the sale.

2. If more than a minor portion but less than all of the property is leased back (between 10 and 90%) *and* a profit is realized on the sale, such profit shall be recognized to the extent that it exceeds the present value of the minimum lease payments (operating leases) or the recorded amount of the leased asset (capital leases).

3. If the fair value of the leased property is less than book value at the date of the sale and leaseback, a loss shall be recognized for the difference.

In classifying leases in sale and leaseback transactions the usual criteria are applicable except that for purchaser/lessors, only the direct financing classification is permissible for capital leases.

Special Areas: Subleases

Lessor. Accounting by a lessor is not affected by a lessee's sublease agreements. If, however, the lessor enters a new agreement with a new lessee as a substitute for the original lessee, the original lease is treated as a termination (see above) and the new lease is classified under the basic rules.

Lessee: When a lessee is relieved of primary obligation under a lease, the lessee shall account for the event as a termination (see above) and shall treat any loss contingency under a secondary obligation in accordance with FASB 5 (Sec. C59).

When a lessee subleases the property and remains primarily liable under the original lease, the following accounting is required:

1. Original lease is a capital lease:
   a. If the original lease was classified as a capital lease because it transferred ownership or contained a bargain purchase option, the sublease shall be subjected to the same classification criteria as an original lease. If the sublease is classified as a sales-type or direct financing lease, the "cost" of the property to the original lessee shall be the unamortized balance of the leased asset under the original lease.
   b. If the original lease did not transfer ownership or contain a bargain purchase option, the sublease shall be classified a direct financing lease only if the sublease covers 75% or more of the economic life of the asset and meets the additional criteria for lessors (collectibility and no uncertainties). If the original lease and the sublease are part of a single transaction, the sublease criteria shall also include the 90%-of-fair-value test.
2. Original lease is an operating lease: If the original lease is an operating lease, the sublease must also be an operating lease.

The original lessee shall continue to account for the obligation under the original lease in the same manner regardless of whether the sublease is an operating lease or a capital lease.

Special Areas: Leveraged Leases

Special accounting requirements for leveraged leases apply only to the lessor and the lessee must account for the lease in the same way as other leases. A leveraged lease must meet the following four conditions:

1. The lease meets the general definition of a direct financing lease.
2. There are three parties to the transaction: a lessee, a lessor, and a long-term creditor.
3. The creditor is not a general creditor of the lessor but may have recourse to the leased asset and unpaid rentals. The financing is large enough to leave the lessor with significant leverage.
4. The lessor's net investment (defined below) generally declines in the earlier years of the lease and rises in later years.

Investment in a leveraged lease, reported net of the debt to the long-term creditor, is composed of the following:

1. Rents receivable less principal and interest on the debt, plus
2. Investment credit to be realized, plus
3. Estimated residual value of the asset, plus or minus
4. Deferred income to be allocated to income over the lease term

Income from the leveraged lease shall be determined by calculating a rate of return on the net investment and cash flows over the lease term. The rate shall assign income to years when the net investment is positive. The net investment will be increased or decreased by the cash flows and the income realized.

Losses must be recognized at inception of the lease if expected cash receipts are less than the initial investment and at any other time during the lease term that a loss is indicated. The lease must be reviewed annually and any necessary revisions must be reflected in a revised rate of return for the entire lease period with necessary gains or losses from such revision taken to current income. The only exception here is that the estimated residual value of the asset must not be increased.

Deferred taxes related to the leveraged lease must be reported apart from the lease in accordance with APB Opinion 11 (Sec. I24, I28). The income statement must separately reflect income from the lease, taxes on this income, and recognition of investment credit. Footnote disclosure is required of the components of the net investment balance when leveraged leasing is a significant part of the lessor's financial position or results of operations.

Interpretation 19

This interpretation deals with a lessee's guarantee of residual value of leased property and the conditions under which minimum lease payments are affected.

1. An agreement to compensate a lessor for a residual value deficiency resulting from physical use of the property is not deemed to be a residual value guarantee.
2. Where the lessee's maximum obligation to compensate for a residual value deficiency is less than the total residual value, the minimum lease payments shall include only the lessee's maximum obligation.

3. A third-party guarantee of residual value may reduce the lessee's minimum lease payments only if the lessor releases the lessee from any claim for a deficiency.

Interpretation 21

Leases acquired in a business combination must maintain their original classification unless the leases are modified pursuant to the combination, in which case the basic provisions of FASB 13 relating to modification of leases applies.

Interpretation 23

All of the following conditions must be met to classify a lease as an operating lease under the special rule for property owned by a governmental unit:
The leased property:
1. Is owned by government
2. Is part of a larger property
3. Is permanent and not movable
4. Cannot be purchased
5. Is not transferred by the lease
6. May be withdrawn by cancellation of the lease

If all of these conditions are not met, a lease is subject to the normal classification criteria.

Interpretation 24

When part of a building is leased, fair value may be determined from sales of similar property, construction costs, appraisals, estimated replacement costs, and other reasonable evidence.

Interpretation 26

When a lessee purchases a leased asset, the difference between the book value of the lease obligation and the purchase price must be an adjustment to the book value of the asset.

Interpretation 27

An original lessee is not prohibited from recognizing a loss on disposal or subletting of leased property.

When the sublease is part of a disposal of a segment of a business, any gain or loss is determined by considering estimated cash flows from the lease and sublease and any asset and obligation balances related to the original lease.

Sources for this topic in FASB *Accounting Standards: Current Text*:
>   APB Opinion 29
>   FASB Interpretation 30

PROFILE:

- Dissimilar assets transferred should be valued at fair value of the asset surrendered (or fair value of asset received if more clearly evident); gain or loss should be recognized.
- Similar assets transferred are recorded at book value. Loss is recorded if asset value is impaired. Gains are recorded only when cash is received and then only proportionally.

DISCLOSURE:

- In the period in which a nonmonetary transaction occurs, the financial statements must disclose the nature of the transaction, the basis of accounting for the assets transferred, and gains or losses recognized.

This opinion deals with transactions involving exchanges and transfers where neither party exchanges monetary assets or liabilities and therefore the usual objective valuation basis is missing. The opinion focuses on the mutual exchange of assets or liabilities (reciprocal transfer) as well as a transfer of nonmonetary assets without reciprocity by the other party (nonreciprocal transfer).

The basic principle for valuing nonmonetary transactions is fair value of the asset surrendered at the date of the exchange with recognition of gain or loss on the asset surrendered. If fair value of the asset received is more readily determinable, this value should be used. If fair value of neither asset exchanged is reasonably determinable, the book value of the asset surrendered may be the only alternative for valuing the transaction.

If the exchange does not result in the termination of an earning process (i.e., similar assets are exchanged), the valuation to be used is the book value of the asset surrendered with no gain or loss recorded. The only exception to this rule is the case where cash is *received* on the exchange and a gain is indicated. Losses should always be recognized and gains should not be recognized by the party paying cash. The gain recognized by the recipient of cash is that portion of the gain that cash bears to the total consideration received. In formula form:

$$\text{Recognized gain} = \text{indicated gain} \times \frac{\text{cash}}{\text{cash} + \text{other assets}}$$

Nonreciprocal transfer of assets to owners of an enterprise should be based on recorded amounts if the transaction is a spin-off, liquidation, or reversal of a business combination. All other nonreciprocal transfers should use fair values of assets surrendered.

When one or more nonmonetary transactions have occurred in an accounting period, the financial statements should disclose the nature, basis of accounting, and gains or losses for the transactions.

Interpretation 30

Involuntary conversions of nonmonetary assets to monetary assets are considered monetary transactions, and gain or loss should be recorded regardless of ultimate disposition of the funds. Such gain or loss requires interperiod tax allocation if treated in a different period for tax purposes.

When the monetary assets are to be received in the next period, the gain or loss should be determined following FASB 5, Accounting for Contingencies (Sec. C59).

Sources for this topic in FASB *Accounting Standards: Current Text*:
   APB Opinion 8
   FASB Statement 36
   FASB Interpretation 3
   FASB Technical Bulletin 81–3

PROFILE:

- APB Opinion 8 covers written and implied plans which provide, ordinarily, for monthly pension benefits for retired employees. The practice of paying benefits on an individual basis (not uniformly for all employees) is not a plan as covered by this opinion. The opinion applies to insured, trust fund, and uninsured plans and it applies to defined benefit, defined contribution, and deferred compensation plans (if equivalent to a pension plan).
- FASB Interp. 3 deals with the effect of ERISA on pension accounting.

DISCLOSURE:

- FASB Statement 36 summarizes all disclosures required for pension plans.

APB Opinion 8

Basic Accounting

1. Accounting for pension plans is not discretionary.
2. All costs of the plan must be charged to income after adoption of the plan.
3. Annual pension provision must be determined from an acceptable actuarial cost method limited by a minimum and a maximum.

    Minimum: Normal cost (actuarially determined cost for current year)

    + an interest equivalent for unfunded prior service cost
    + a charge for vested benefits, if applicable

    An addition to the minimum must be made for vested benefits if there has not been a reduction during the year of at least 5% of the amount that vested benefits exceeds the pension fund adjusted for accruals, deferrals, and prepayments. The vested benefits charge then must be the lower of the amount necessary to bring this reduction up to 5% or the amount necessary to bring the total pension provision for the year to the total of the following items:

    a. Normal cost
    b. 2½% of past service cost (unless already expensed)
    c. 2½% of prior service cost changes (unless expensed)
    d. Interest on unfunded pension costs

    Maximum: Normal cost

    + 10% of past service cost (unless already expensed)
    + 10% of prior service cost changes (unless expensed)
    + Interest on unfunded pension costs

4. The difference between charges to income and payments to the fund must be classified on the balance sheet as either prepaid or accrued pension costs. Where a legal obligation exists in excess of amounts accrued or paid, such excess must be reported as both a deferred charge and a liability.

Actuarial Cost Methods

Most actuarial cost methods developed by actuaries to measure pension costs are acceptable for accounting purposes as long as they are a systematic and rational approach to cost measurement and they are consistently applied. One actuarial cost method that is not acceptable for accounting purposes is the terminal funding method; the pay-as-you-go method, which is not an actuarial cost method, is also not acceptable for accounting purposes.

Actuarial Gains and Losses

Actuarial gains and losses, including *realized* investment gains and losses, must be distributed to the current and future years using a period of from ten to twenty years.

If actuarial gains and losses occur from a single event unrelated to operation of the pension plan (e.g., plant closing or merger) they must be recognized immediately.

Unrealized gains and losses should affect the pension provision in a reasonable manner so as not to give too much importance to short-term market fluctuations.

When investment gains and losses (realized or unrealized) relate to variable annuities accounting recognition is required only to the extent that such gains and losses do not affect retirement benefits.

Employees Included in Cost Calculations

All employees whom it is reasonable to expect to participate in the benefits of the plan shall be included in the cost calculations, except that an allowance for expected turnover may be recognized.

Miscellaneous Topics

More Than One Plan.   Firms with several pension plans need not use the same actuarial cost method for all plans, but the accounting for each plan must conform to the requirements of this opinion.

Defined Contribution Plans.   For this type of plan, where benefits of the plan derive from contributions which are arrived at by formula, pension expense must equal the contribution.

Insured Plans.   The insurance aspects of these plans are really forms of funding and thus should not affect pension provisions.

Effect of Funding.   Pension cost provision for the current year must be increased by an interest factor equivalent to interest on the excess of total prior year provisions over amounts funded.

Income Taxes.   Tax allocation is required for timing differences.

Disclosure.   Revised disclosure requirements are spelled out in FASB Statement 36 (see below).

Change in Accounting Method.   Changes in accounting for pension provisions are to be treated as changes in estimates. This means that the effect on prior years of the change must be treated prospectively in the current year and applicable future years.

Interpretation 3

ERISA generally has no effect on the maximum and minimum limits for pension accounting. Any changes made to comply with ERISA must affect pension expense for the periods subsequent to the changes.

If it appears that eventual requirements for compliance with ERISA will have a material effect on the pension provision, funding, or vested benefits, an estimate of such effect shall be disclosed.

ERISA should result in accounting recognition only if:

1. Minimum funding is not achieved and a waiver for underfunding is not obtained. In this event the underfunded amount must be reported as a liability.
2. If it is clear that a plan is to be terminated in the future, any excess of the liability of the terminated plan over funded amounts must be accrued.

FASB Statement 36

All pension plans shall be disclosed in financial statements or notes with the following minimum information:

1. Identification of plans and employees covered
2. Accounting and funding policies for the plan
3. The fiscal period pension expense
4. Information to aid in comparability among periods presented when changes in accounting methods or changes in the plan have occurred

For plans classified as defined benefit plans (as distinguished from defined contribution plans), the following additional disclosures are required:

1. The present value (actuarially determined) of both vested and non-vested benefits
2. Net assets of the plan to provide benefits
3. The discount rate used to determine the present values of vested and nonvested benefits
4. The date used to determine all of the information above

If this additional information cannot be determined, disclosure shall include the reasons it is not provided and the original disclosure requirements of APB Opinion 8 shall apply.

Sources for this topic in FASB *Accounting Standards: Current Text*:
   ARB 43, Chap. 7A; ARB 46

PROFILE:
   - Accounting for the readjustment:
      1. Assets shall be written down to fair market value.
      2. The write-off shall be charged to earned surplus, if any, and the balance shall be charged against additional paid in capital.
   - Accounting following readjustment:
      1. No retained earnings shall survive the readjustment. Retained earnings subsequent to readjustment shall be dated as arising since the readjustment.
      2. Accounting principles following readjustment shall be the same as for any new entity.
   - Dating of retained earnings is not necessary after ten years from the date of readjustment, and in unusual cases it may be permissible to discontinue such dating prior to ten years.

DISCLOSURE:
   - No special requirements

Sources for this topic in FASB *Accounting Standards: Current Text*:
  ARB 43, Chap. 1A
  FASB Statement 57

PROFILE:

- Receivables from officers, employees and affiliates must not be included with trade receivables but must be reported separately.
- Material related-party transactions must be disclosed.

DISCLOSURE:

- Where material transactions have occurred between related parties financial statements shall include the following disclosures:

  1. The nature of the relationship

  2. A description and dollar amount of the transactions for each period an income statement is issued

  3. Receivables or payables with the related parties at the balance sheet date

- Representations shall not imply that related party transactions were equivalent to arm's-length transactions unless this can be demonstrated.
- Regardless of related party transactions, the nature of any control relationship shall be disclosed if the reporting entity's results of operations or financial position can significantly be influenced by such related party.

Sources for this topic in FASB *Accounting Standards: Current Text*:

FASB Statement 2

FASB Interpretation 6

FASB Technical Bulletin 79-2

PROFILE:

- This Statement defines (with examples) activities considered to be research and development for accounting purposes and specifies that such costs must be charged to expense when incurred.

DISCLOSURE:

- Total research and development expense for the period shall be disclosed.

This Statement specifies that costs identified as "research and development" (R&D) are to be expensed in the period in which they are incurred. Exceptions to this rule include R&D conducted under contracts with other parties and activities that are specifically unique to the extractive process, such as exploration, drilling, and mining.

Following are examples for classification purposes of activities which are R&D and which are not R&D for purposes of this Statement.

Research and Development	*Not Research and Development*
1. Laboratory search for new knowledge	1. Engineering after start of production
2. Search for applications of knowldege	2. Quality control and troubleshooting during production
3. Design, testing, or modification of possible products or processes	3. Routine tooling
4. All work related to prototypes and models	4. Routine refinements of designs, products, and processes
5. All work related to tooling for new technologies	5. All normal costs of production facilities
6. All work related to subproduction-level pilot plants	
7. All preproduction engineering on products	

Costs to be included in research and development expense are:

1. Materials, equipment, and facilities
2. Salaries, wages, and related personnel costs
3. Purchased intangibles
4. Contracted services
5. Indirect costs

If these costs have future uses (for R&D or otherwise), they shall be capitalized and amortized as appropriate. Costs incurred for a specific project which have no alternative future uses must be expensed as incurred. Indirect costs shall include a reasonable amount for nondirect costs but shall not include any general and administrative costs that are unrelated to research and development.

Disclosure: Financial statements shall indicate the amount of R&D expensed each period. Regulated enterprises shall, in addition, indicate the amount of R&D capitalized if R&D is deferred and shall disclose their accounting policy for R&D, including the basis for amortization of amounts capitalized.

Interpretation 6

Costs incurred in the development of computer software shall be classified as research and development or not using the same criteria as those applied to other costs. The reason for incurring the costs and their relationship to contracts, products, and production should indicate their classification in accordance with FASB Statement 2.

Sources for this topic in FASB *Accounting Standards: Current Text*:
    ARB 43, Chap. 1A; ARB 51
    FASB Statement 5

PROFILE:
  • Unrealized profit must not be taken into income directly
       nor should unrealized profit absorb charges that
       should be made to income.
  • Consolidated retained earnings should not include any
       retained earnings of a purchased subsidiary recorded
       as of the date of acquisition.

DISCLOSURE:
  • No special requirements

Sources for this topic in FASB *Accounting Standards: Current Text*:
ARB 43,
APB Opinion 10
FASB Statement 48

PROFILE:

- The installment method of recognizing revenue is not acceptable. Revenue must be recognized upon sale, with appropriate provision for uncollectible accounts. Only in very exceptional circumstances where there is no reasonable basis for assessing collectibility may the installment method or the cost recovery method be used.

- FASB Statement 48 specifies six requirements that must be met before revenue may be recorded at the date of a sale when the buyer has the right to return the product.

DISCLOSURE:

- No special requirements

FASB Statement 48

When sales are made to buyers who are granted the right to return the product, revenue shall be recognized at the date of the sale *only if all* of the following are met:

1. The selling price is established at the date of the sale.
2. The seller has been paid or the buyer's obligation to pay is not contingent on the buyer's resale of the product.
3. The buyer's obligation is not affected by loss or damage of the product.
4. The buyer is an entity independent of the seller.
5. The seller has no obligation to affect the resale of the product by the buyer.
6. Future returns can be reasonably estimated.

If revenue and related costs are not recognized because all of the conditions above were not met, revenue and cost must be recognized at the earlier of: (a) meeting all of the conditions, or (b) expiration of the return privilege.

Sources for this topic in FASB *Accounting Standards: Current Text:*
    FASB Statements 14, 18, 21, 24, 30
    FASB Technical Bulletins 79–4, –5, –8

PROFILE:
- Segment information about industries, foreign operations, and major customers is required for all publicly held enterprises. The information required is revenue, profit or loss, and assets for reportable segments.

DISCLOSURE:
- All of the information required by this Statement are supplemental disclosures to basic financial statements.

Publicly held companies are required to report supplemental segment information about industries, foreign business, and customers when complete annual financial statements are issued. Segment information is not required for:

1. Interim financial statements (FASB 18)
2. Nonpublic enterprises (FASB 21)
3. Complete sets of financial statements included with a primary reporting entity's financial statements (FASB 24)

Segment information must be based on the same generally accepted accounting principles used in the primary financial statements, including the disaggregations described below. Enterprises are not required to report segment information for investees accounted for by the equity method except to identify the industry and geographic area in which the investee operates.

Transactions between constituents that are eliminated for consolidation must be reported as part of the segment information and the total segment information must be reconciled with the consolidated financial statements.

Industry Information

This Statement requires classification of industry segments, selection of segments for which disclosures are required, identification of information for reporting, and presentation of the segment information.

1. Identification of industry segments. An industry segment is a component of an enterprise that operates to make a profit from transactions with unrelated entities. The component may be a division, subsidiary, department, or other form of profit center. Industry classification may follow the Standard Industrial Classification or other reasonable scheme. Since the criterion for identification of segments is imprecise, management judgment is an important factor in the identification process.
2. Selection of reportable segments. Segment information may be required for any segment that meets at least one of the following tests:
   a. Revenue: Gross revenue of the segment is 10% or more of the gross revenue of the entity. Gross revenue here means revenue before intersegment eliminations.

    b. Profit or loss: The segment profit or loss is 10% or more of:

        (1) Total profit for segments earning a profit, or

        (2) Total losses for segments incurring losses, as appropriate

    c. Assets: The segment's assets are 10% or more of total assets identifiable by segment.

3. After these tests are applied, two further factors must be considered before the list of reportable segments is finalized:

    a. Comparability of segment information should be considered in evaluating the initial results of the revenue, profit, and asset tests. The objective is not to include or exclude segments because of seemingly temporary variations in values used in applying the tests.

    b. The total revenue to be reported by the segments must be at least 75% of the total sales to unrelated parties. If total revenue of segments identified from the revenue, profit, and asset tests do not equal this 75% test, additional segments must be identified until 75% is reached. These additional segments may have to be combined when the number of segments exceeds a practical limit of about ten segments.

4. Information to be presented. The following information must be reported for each reportable segment and in total for all segments that are not reportable:

    a. Revenue: Separate figures shall be reported for sales to unaffiliated customers and transfers to other segments. Pricing of the intersegment transfers may be at the values used internally, but the method of accounting for these transactions should be disclosed.

    b. Profitability: Operating profit or loss shall be reported. This profit or loss is defined as gross segment revenue minus operating expenses and allocated nontraceable expenses which have benefited the segment. Specifically excluded from determination of segment profit are corporate revenues and expenses, income taxes, interest, income of investees, and all items reported on the income statement below income from continuing operations.

    c. Identifiable assets: The amount of assets employed shall be reported. This includes assets directly used by a segment and allocation of assets shared by segments. Assets not used in segment operations should be excluded. Valuation of assets is to be net of applicable allowance accounts.

    d. Other disclosures: The following information shall also be reported for each reportable segment:

        (1) Total depreciation, depletion, and amortization expense

        (2) Capital expenditures

        (3) Equity in income and investment in vertically integrated segment investees (if any)

        (4) Effect on operating profit of a segment of changes in accounting principles (if any)

5. Methods of presentation. The format for segment disclosures may be within the statements (with explanatory footnotes), completely in the notes to the statements, or in a separate schedule referenced as an integral part of the financial statements.

Foreign Operations Information

An entity shall report informtion on its foreign operations if either of the following tests is met:

1. Revenue of the foreign operations from transactions with nonaffiliates is 10% or more of total revenue of the entity, or
2. Assets of the foreign operation are 10% or more of consolidated assets.

Further, the disclosures are required separately for operations in each geographic area that meets either of the foregoing tests. Total foreign and domestic operations must be reconciled to the appropriate consolidated totals.

The information that must be presented for the foreign and domestic dichotomy are revenues, operating profit or loss, and assets as defined above under the industry segment requirements. The methods of presentation also may take any of the forms indicated for disclosure of industry segment information.

Major Customers

An entity shall disclose the amount of revenue derived from any customer that exceeds 10% of total revenue. A customer is defined as any group under common control and any governmental unit (whether federal, state, local, or foreign). The identity of the customer may be protected, but the industry segment generating the revenue must be identified.

Changes in Accounting or Segment Classification

Previously issued segment information that is reissued for comparative purposes must be retroactively restated when either:

1. Complete financial statements are restated for changes in accounting or to reflect a pooling of interests, or
2. The entity revises its industry or foreign operation groupings for the current segment information.

Sources for this topic in FASB *Accounting Standards: Current Text*:
  ARB 43, Chap. 10A

PROFILE:

- This chapter presents several types of periods for accruing real and personal property taxes, but the preferable method is monthly accrual using the fiscal period of the taxing jurisdiction.
- The accrued liability must be current and labeled "estimated" if a material uncertainty exists as to the amount.
- These taxes are usually expenses, except where capitalized while property is being developed.
- Adjustments to accruals of prior years must affect current income.

DISCLOSURE:

- No special requirements

Sources for this topic in FASB *Accounting Standards: Current Text*:
   APB Opinion 12

PROFILE:
- Accumulated allowances for depreciation and depletion and valuation allowances such as those for receivables and investments should be deducted from the assets to which they relate. (They should not be placed on the credit side of the balance sheet.)

DISCLOSURE:
- None required

Sources for this topic in FASB *Accounting Standards: Current Text*:
FASB Statement 51

PROFILE:

- Cable companies must establish a prematurity period for the time while construction and revenue earning occurs simultaneously.
- A formula is developed for partial recognition of costs during this prematurity period and rules are established for capitalizing system costs.

DISCLOSURE:

- No special requirements

Prematurity Period

Management of the cable television company shall determine the beginning and end of a prematurity period prior to earning revenue from subscribers. This prematurity period is that time when the system is under construction and revenue is being generated. Such prematurity period may not be longer than two years (except in large urban markets where it may be justified) and usually will be shorter than two years. Once determined, the prematurity period shall not be altered except in very unusual circumstances.

The part of the total system that is in the prematurity period, and which can be clearly identified, shall be accounted for separately. Generally, this identifiable part of the system will exhibit most of the following attributes:

    a. geographical identity distinct from other parts of the system

    b. equipment differences, such as separate receivers

    c. different timing of construction start-up or marketing

    d. separate investment decisions

    e. separate accounting, budgeting and forecasting.

Costs incurred for the total system may be charged to that part of the system in the prematurity period only if specifically identified with the operations of that part. Capitalized costs for the part in the prematurity period shall be separately evaluated for recoverability.

Accounting during the prematurity period shall be as follows:

    a. costs of the cable television plant shall be capitalized

    b. general, administrative and subscriber-related costs shall be expensed

    c. programming and other system costs incurred to complete the system shall be accounted for prospectively by expensing the current portion and capitalizing the portion that will benefit future operations, as determined below.

Each month during the prematurity period a fraction shall be developed to determine the portion of that month's programming and other systems costs that should be expensed and to determine the portion of capitalized costs that should be depreciated and amortized. This fraction shall have a numerator which is the largest of:

a. the number of subscribers expected for the month based on the estimate at the beginning of the prematurity period, or

b. the number of subscribers which would be added each month if the total expected subscribers were added evenly over the prematurity period, or

c. the actual number of subscribers added to date.

The denominator of the fraction is the total number of subscribers expected by the end of the prematurity period.

Expense of programming and other system costs incurred for the month shall be those costs times the fraction developed above. The balance of these costs shall be capitalized. Depreciation and amortization of capitalized costs for the month shall be determined by multiplying monthly depreciation and amortization of expected total capitalized cost at the end of the prematurity period by the fraction developed above. The depreciation method should be that method which will be used after the prematurity period.

Interest to be capitalized shall be determined in accordance with FASB 34 (Sec. I67).

Other Accounting Requirements

Costs that have been capitalized during the prematurity period should be amortized over the same period used to depreciate the main cable television plant.